WHAT OTHERS ARE SAYING

"Finally! An employee rights attorney who tells it like it is! Amazingly readable. Sessions has filled his book with golden nuggets of wisdom and advice for both managers and employees."

—Bruce Hyland
Co-author, *Reflections for the Workplace*

"Very informative. Sessions is the premier authority on the legal rights of employees. It's a great resource presented in a no-nonsense format."

—Rob Shannon
Senior Editor, Cass Communications Inc.,
Career development publications

"Well-written and easy to understand."

—Elena Perez
California NOW

"A treasure of enjoyable reading and useful reference. Very helpful comparisons of government agencies."

—Stuart M. Kaye
Former trial attorney, California Labor Commissioner

"This book should be classified as the "bible" of employee rights in California. In fact, if I were a chief executive officer or human resources director for a company, I would require all my managers to read Employee Rights in California. Knowledge of the law can prevent many problems—and save your company money and costly litigation.

"Don D. Sessions is an encyclopedia of knowledge on employee rights. Employee Rights in California reflects Sessions' vast knowledge and broad experience. It presents a balanced and very practical approach to dealing with employee disputes. Sessions understands both points of view and tries to resolve the issues with minimal conflict. Unlike most attorneys, he is not litigation-happy. He looks at the big picture and encourages employees to be practical and consider the consequences of any action or threatened action they may take. He often warns an employee not to win the battle while losing the war.

"On the other hand, when litigation or other legal action is clearly called for, Sessions does not hesitate to recommend these strong measures to fully protect the employee's rights.

"Employee Rights in California is easy to read, full of information about just about every kind of job-related problem and includes a valuable section on resources employees can turn to when they have a problem. It is a bargain. I highly recommend it."

—Ray A. Cohn
Public Relations Director, Forty Plus of Southern California

EMPLOYEE RIGHTS
IN CALIFORNIA

DON D. SESSIONS
Employee Rights Attorney

PRETIUM PRESS

Mission Viejo, California

EMPLOYEE RIGHTS IN CALIFORNIA

Pretium Press
23456 Madero, Suite 170
Mission Viejo, CA 92691
(949) 206-6825

Copyright © 1998 by Don D. Sessions

Publisher's Cataloging-in-Publication Data
Sessions, Don D., 1949-
Employee Rights in California / Don D. Sessions.
— 1st ed. p. cm.
Includes index.
ISBN 0-9658449-1-9
1. Labor laws and legislation — California.
2. Employee rights — California.
3. Labor laws and legislation — United States.
4. Employee rights — California — Miscellanea.
I. Title. II Title: Los Angeles Times (Firm)
KFC556.S47 1998
344.794'01
QB197-41501
Library of Congress Catalog Card Number 97-92845

Printed in the United States of America
Second printing, 2000

PREFACE

"Shop Talk" has been a popular feature in the Sunday Business Section of the *Los Angeles Times* for many years. It features questions on employment rights submitted by readers, and answers by employee rights attorney Don D. Sessions and others.

Every few weeks up to 16 lawyers and law clerks at Mr. Sessions' law firm discuss, research and evaluate real-life questions received from the editors of the *Los Angeles Times*. Varying points of view from both the employer and employee perspectives are considered. They eventually agree on the most correct "legal" and "practical" solution. Mr. Sessions' written answer, subject to limitations of publishing space, then appears a few weeks later in the "Shop Talk" column of the Sunday Business Section.

This book is organized for interest and ease of use. The questions are grouped into appropriate topics from pre-hiring to post-firing. There is a short description of each question along with the actual title which appeared in the *Los Angeles Times*. The answer then follows with occasional paraphrased quotes. Some portions of the questions and answers as originally published have been deleted to fit this format. The Appendix supplements these answers with additional information on free services and seminars.

This book was written because it is needed. Although there are many general books on national employment law, there are few, if any, combining legal and practical advice for California employees.

*This book was written because
it is needed.*

TABLE OF CONTENTS

Discrimination

Whistle-Blowing

Slander

Privacy

Unemployment

Recourse

Appendix

ACKNOWLEDGMENTS

This book would not have been possible without the loving encouragement of my family.

I gratefully acknowledge the contribution of all the attorneys and law clerks at our firm who weekly evaluate, research and discuss "Shop Talk" questions from the *Los Angeles Times* with me. Their insights have helped me write better answers than I could have done alone.

Thanks must be given to the many employees who wrote to the Times. We have all learned more because they shared part of themselves. There would be no "Shop Talk" without them.

For years now, the editors of the *Los Angeles Times* have helped its readers with "Shop Talk." They should be congratulated for the service they provide.

The tears, trauma and financial devastation of thousands of employees I have represented over the years give my practice its soul. Being a "crusader" for their rights in the media, my law practice and my law school courses has been my heartfelt privilege.

Don D. Sessions
Mission Viejo, California

ABOUT THE AUTHOR

 Employee rights attorney Don D. Sessions has answered questions from readers of the *Los Angeles Times* "Shop Talk" column for many years.

He graduated from Loyola Law School in Los Angeles in 1976. His early career was spent representing businesses, often in disputes with employees. Since then, he has exclusively represented employee rights. As the need for his services increased, his firm expanded to a staff of 27 employees, becoming one of the largest employee rights firms in California.

He is co-editor of the ABA-sponsored supplement to the eminent treatise Employment Discrimination Law, a frequent contributor to the Orange County Register, a continuing columnist for EEO Bimonthly Equal Opportunity Career Journal, and co-author/reviewer for pamphlets on employment law produced and sold by the *Los Angeles Times*. His comments and articles have been published in magazines including Time, Newsweek, Business Week, U.S. News and World Report, The Wall Street Journal, The Atlantic Monthly, Forbes, Worth, Self, Inc., and National Business Employment Weekly.

Mr. Sessions has given hundreds of seminars and appears on television or radio programs monthly. He is the chairman of the Employment Law Section of the Orange County Bar Association. As an adjunct professor at Western State University College of Law, Mr. Sessions has taught courses on employee rights. He wrote and published one of the few law school texts on wrongful termination law. Martindale-Hubbell, the national attorney rating service, gave Mr. Sessions its highest ranking of "very high to preeminent" based on the opinions of local judges and attorneys.

WARNING-DISCLAIMER

This book is designed to give information in regard to the subject matter covered. It is sold with the understanding that the publisher and author are not engaged in rendering legal, accounting or other professional services. If legal or other expert assistance is required, the services of a competent professional should be sought.

The answers listed in this book were limited by publishing requirements and frequent inability to fully clarify the facts behind the questions. Thus, the responses are not comprehensive and should not be relied on as if they apply to all situations. Additional information and resources have been listed in the Appendix.

Laws continually change. Accordingly, this book contains information only current to the date it was originally published. Statute of limitations deadlines, some even less than a year from the date of a wrongful act, may prevent enforcement of employee rights unless appropriate legal action is taken. Thus, the reader is advised to promptly obtain the most up-to-date legal advice from an attorney.

The purpose of this book is to educate and entertain. The publisher and author shall have no liability or responsibility to any person or entity as to any loss or damage caused, or alleged to be caused, directly or indirectly by the information contained in this book.

If you do not desire to be bound by the above, you may return this book to the publisher for a full refund.

Although there are many general books on national employment law, there are few, if any, combining practical and legal advice for California employees.

INTRODUCTION

Few Rights Over a Long History

Employment rights and relationships are nothing new. Work has been around a long time. It started eons ago with our hunter/gatherer ancestors. Eventually they found mutual advantage to seeking food in a group. Through the millennia, group leaders emerged, exercised control with resulting city-states, and later nations. Slavery and wars between nations arose, at least in part, out of the desire of one person or group to control another's productivity and labor. Employees have not enjoyed an abundance of rights throughout history. They worked at the whim and under the conditions imposed on them by their masters. Issues of employment and labor have been at the center of human existence and relationships since the very beginning, and continue to this day.

More Rights in the Last Century

In the 1800s there were few laws governing child labor, safety, hours, benefits, and other conditions of employment. In the early 1900s, these injustices were detailed in books such as Upton Sinclair's *The Jungle*, which exposed the deplorable working conditions of the meat-packing plants in the eastern United States.

In the last century, employees finally began to gain significant rights. In the 1930s, laws were enacted which provided important safeguards for the organization and rights of unions. A minimum 40-hour work week was legislated not only to prevent abuses to workers, but to provide incentive to employers to employ more workers.

More Rights Than Ever in Recent Years

In the last 30 years, employees have gained more rights than ever before. The Civil Rights Act of 1964 prohibited discrimination on the basis of race, color, religion, sex or national origin. Age was added to the list of protected categories in 1967. These statutes provided a model for many of the states' anti-discrimination laws.

In the 1970s, further employee rights legislation was enacted regarding safety, retirement plans, and veteran status. In 1988, Congress passed laws to provide mandatory notice or compensation for workers losing jobs due to plant closures. The 1990s have seen comprehensive amendments to the Civil Rights Act and passage of new laws to protect people with disabilities and to provide mandatory leave and reinstatement for family and medical reasons.

States vary widely in the type of protection they give to workers. With federal rules establishing the minimum standards, many states have provided even more protection for workers. By the close of the 1980s, most states had adopted some form of exception to the employment at-will doctrine, which allows employers to terminate a worker's employment even without cause.

California's Leadership

California has given employees more protection through laws and court decisions than any other state in the country. Our example sets the pattern for other states to follow. Even the federal government evaluates our progressive laws for possible national application. The future looks bright for employee rights in California. Every year, legislation and judicial rulings provide additional protection for workers.

Challenge for California Employees

Everyone is an employee or cares about someone who is. We spend most of our weekday time at work. People even define themselves by their occupation. Loss of a job is said to be the most traumatic life experience after death of a loved one or a divorce. Yet people know remarkably little about the rights that govern this important part of their lives. Furthermore, they do not know how to balance legal and practical advice.

While all the questions, answers and supplementary information in this book may be interesting, they will be of little use unless actually applied in the workplace. There is no doubt that knowledge can equal power. Understanding the concepts of this book is at least a start to controlling one's work life and reaping the happiness and financial rewards that should follow.

Understanding the concepts of this book is at least a start to controlling one's work life and reaping the happiness and financial rewards that should follow.

PROMISES

1

POLICY PROMISES

At-Will Employment Can Be Overcome

Q On the majority of today's employment applications there is an at-will clause regarding termination, which all employees must sign before being hired. What can an individual do in order to have this labor clause, which I think is unfair, removed?

—R.F., Santa Ana

A The doctrine that employees can be terminated "at-will"—with or without a reason—has existed for more than 100 years. Montana is the only state that has a "just cause" termination statute. In all other states, the policy has been followed by the courts. In addition, California and Georgia have statutes permitting such terminations.

There are many things that can be done to contest such a policy: write your state legislator to continue attempts to abolish the law; seek employment in a state where the doctrine does not exist or where it is not as well established as in California. If you have sufficient bargaining power as an employee, insist that the employer delete it from your employment agreement. Document and confirm in writing any promises by your employer of continued employment or progressive discipline which might be enough to nullify any other self-serving, at-will clause.

> *The doctrine that employees can be terminated "at will" has existed for more than 100 years. This does not necessarily mean you can be fired for any reason.*

The most important thing to realize is that even if you think you are an at-will employee, it does not necessarily mean you can be fired for any reason. Most states have exceptions to such a rule, such as employment actions involving discrimination, retaliation against whistle-blowers, or an implied contract based on other factors requiring good cause for termination.

If you have an employment problem, government agencies will help you with discrimination (such as the state Department of Fair Employment and Housing or the federal Equal Employment Opportunity Commision), wage claims or retaliation (State Labor Commissioner or federal Department of Labor), but not with breach of contract or at-will disputes. An employment adviser, such as a personnel recruiter you hire, or an attorney may be helpful in negotiating a good employment contract before you are hired or in pursing your rights when they have been violated.

2

PAY

PROMISES

Making Company Honor Pay Promise Can Be Tricky

Q My company took over the office about two months ago. They agreed to pay me the salary I was making and then reneged, so I'm making less than I was before. I want to quit my job because I'm unhappy.

What can I do to get back the difference in salary?

—B.S., Orange County

A Employers must abide by their promises to pay wages. The problem is proving the details and the timing of the promise. Even if the promise was made, you would have to determine the length of time that the new salary would continue in effect.

Employers must abide by their promises to pay wages.

The employers will probably claim that they simply conveyed to you their "hope" and that you knew that they were not going to comply soon thereafter, certainly when you received your first paycheck. If anything, they would argue, you only lost salary for that one pay period until you knew definitely that they would not follow through with their commitments.

The amount of your damages may be minimal. Evaluate whether the difference between the amount they promised and the amount you make is significant enough to warrant legal action.

Thus, even if you can prove that they made the promise, the amount of your damages may be minimal. You need to evaluate whether the difference between the amount that they promised and the amount that you make is significant enough to warrant legal action.

You could either file a claim with the California Labor Commissioner's office, who would investigate your claim for free, file a small claims lawsuit or see an attorney. I would suggest, in any event, that you try to find a replacement job before you complain too strongly.

3
AT-WILL PRETEXT

'Reason Behind Reason' For Firing Important

Q I went to work for a company as an executive secretary to the CEO and vice president of sales.

Their expectations were outlined before I accepted the position. After two weeks on the job, I had nearly fulfilled them when I was called into the Human Resources office and terminated without any reason except that I was still in my one-month probation period. There had been no conflicts, no warnings.

I have never been fired before and I have proof and references that my skills and attitude are top-notch. Do I have legal grounds against this employer?

—S.L., Fountain Valley

A In all likelihood, you were an at-will employee subject to termination with or without cause. Under California law, an at-will employee is not entitled to receive any warnings prior to termination even if performance is perfect.

There is always a chance that you might not be considered an at-will employee, however. It depends whether any written or oral representations were made to you. Evaluate the employee handbook to see what rules were to be followed. If you were given guarantees of being fired only for cause, then such promises should have been followed.

> *Evaluate the employee handbook to see what rules were to be followed.*

Also evaluate if the employer falsely induced you to leave other employment to join this one. Even if you were an at-will employee, you might be able to recover for fraud if you can show that they actually lied.

Also, it is illegal for an employer to discipline, terminate or demote even an at-will employee based on discrimination or retaliation because of certain whistle-blower activity.

> *It is illegal for an employer to discipline an at-will employee because of whistle-blower activity.*

You should check the "reason behind the reason" for your termination. It doesn't really make sense they would let you go if you are as perfect an employee as you say. You might ask some of your fellow employees to ask the boss the real reason you were let go. You might also ask a prospective employer to let you know the results of a reference check to your previous boss.

4

AT-WILL DEADLINES

'At-Will' Employment Has Limits

Q In early 1993, I was recruited by a start-up company in California. Both the human relations person for contract employees and their chief operating officer indicated that "this will be your last job, so go ahead and pay your own relocation; it will pay off in the long run." Another manager at a similar level did receive reimbursement for moving expenses.

I performed the duties as assigned, and after setting up the entire 13 western states, was separated from the company in June 1994. I was told that I was not compatible with my supervisor.

I attempted to discuss this matter with an attorney, who said: "You are not in a protected class. It is not worth the effort to go after them." I am over 50, and I spent a considerable amount to get here. Are there no protections out there for me?

—T.C., Lake Forest

A Over the years, there has been considerable publicity about "at-will" employment. This is the right of the employer to terminate an employee's employment and an employee to quit with or without cause. In California, we have not only case law that supports this doctrine, but statutory law as well.

There are limits to employers simply saying "goodbye." There are several exceptions that require "good cause" before an employee is terminated. The at-will rule does not apply to an employer who discriminates, retaliates for an illegal reason or breaches an expressed or implied contract to terminate only for good cause.

In your situation, there are little facts that hint at discrimination or retaliation for improper purpose. It appears that there is a mysterious double standard in the way they treated you compared to another manager who received reimbursement for moving expenses.

You need to evaluate the real reason behind this difference. Was it because of race, age, sex or some other discriminatory reason? Also evaluate the alleged incompatibility with your supervisor. Incompatibility is not good cause for dismissal if it is based on discrimination.

You mentioned that you were over 50. The law protects those who are over 40 from age discrimination if it in fact exists. One evidence of such discrimination might be the younger age of the other manager who was treated more favorably.

The statute of limitations might be a problem. You were separated from the company more than a year ago. Unless you filed a claim with a state or federal agency, your delays might prevent you from claiming discrimination unless a contractual promise was violated.

You can claim fraud, citing false representations initially made to you. It might be difficult to show that they intentionally lied at that time, however.

It should be a lesson to you and others to promptly evaluate potential rights prior to expiration of legal deadlines.

5
FRAUDULENT PROMISES

Fraud Claim Is Shown By Intentional
False Promises

Q I was hired by a company for a salaried position with commission and given a specific sales territory, which was five minutes from my home. The primary reason I left my old job was an excess amount of driving.

After two weeks of training, I was told the territory I thought I would receive had been given to someone else, actually prior to my being hired. My new territory requires driving two hours each way. I don't know if I have any rights in this matter.

—S.F., Fullerton

An employer is liable if it misrepresents terms of employment to a prospective employee who relies on such statements to his or her detriment. If the employer knew that the promise of a certain territory was a material reason for you accepting this new job assignment, then failure to fulfill that promise constitutes breach of contract.

If the employer knew at the time that the promise was made to you that it had no intent to fulfill the promise, as it appears in your case, then the breach of contract might even amount to a fraud claim. Not only could you recover your out-of-pocket wage losses, but also punitive damages.

The key is being able to prove the promise was made to you. Your word against the employer's still may be good enough.

The key here is being able to prove that the promise was in fact made to you. If it is your word against the employer's word, that still may be good enough. It would be better if you could confirm it through another witness or a written document. Additionally, you need to be able to prove that the employer knew that the territory had been assigned to somebody else prior to you being hired and the representations being made to you.

You also will need to show that you adequately communicated to the employer that the specific assignment of territory was an important reason for you accepting the job.

The damages you suffered also affect the value of your claim. If your new job gives you substantially more pay than your old job despite the driving, then you might hesitate to complain too strongly to your employer. However, if the main difference is simply the extent of the driving, then consider your ability to find a replacement job before threatening your employer with legal action.

6

ORAL PROMISES

Company's Oral Promises Could Be Difficult To Prove

Q In 1988 I was recruited by a start-up company. The president offered real estate and moving expenses, as well as stock options, as part of the package to relocate from the Bay Area. But she refused to put most of the offer in writing, citing a trust factor. During my employment, I was persuaded to defer the expenses because the company was not doing as well as planned.

My job was eliminated in May 1991. When I asked for deferred bonus and expenses during my exit interview, I was told that I could sue the company, but that if prospective employers called for references, they would be advised that I had filed a lawsuit against my former employer. It took almost two years to secure a comparable position.

I have since written several times to the founder of the company, with copies to board members and financial backers, but with no tangible results. Do I have a legal recourse against the company?

—J.N.B., Orange

A Promises do not necessarily need to be in writing to be enforceable, although it may be difficult to prove that your company made the oral promises to you.

Ultimately they convinced you to defer the expenses until 1991. At that time, you may have had a claim against them for breach of contract or possibly even fraud. Misrepresentations made to an employee to induce a change of residence can result in a criminal penalty and also double damages.

Misrepresentations made to an employee to induce a change of residence can result in a criminal penalty.

The money should have been paid to you at the time of your termination. When compensation is not appropriately paid on the date of termination, an employee's wages may continue for an additional 30 days as a penalty. Also, a wrongful-termination claim may arise if an employee can show that a job is eliminated in part to avoid the payment of such wages.

It also looks like the company was threatening you with a bad reference. If you have any evidence that they blacklisted you or made any misrepresentation about you to a prospective employer, you could claim triple damages as well as possibly impose a criminal charge on them.

If you have evidence that they blacklisted you, you could claim triple damages.

The biggest problem is that any applicable statute of limitations deadline has long since passed. Even though you had rights, they cannot now be enforced. Hopefully others will learn the lesson that if you think your rights have been violated, you should do something about it promptly.

7

ORAL CONTRACT

*20% Pay Cut for Firm Has Worker
Wondering*

Q Two years ago our employer decided to cut 20% of all salaries because of the recession. He promised to restore the 20% cut as soon as the economy picked up. To date, we are still working for 20% less pay, and our employer is remodeling the building that he owns. Also, we are required to come in on our days off (Saturdays) to learn how to operate new computers he purchased.

Is it legal for him to cut our pay and use the money for other purposes to benefit his own company? Though all of us are salaried, is it legal for him to make it mandatory that we have to learn how to operate new equipment on our days off without pay?

—C.N., Long Beach

A Oral contracts are very difficult to enforce because of vagueness problems. One person says a statement is a promise that means one thing, and to someone else it means something different. To you employees, you feel that promises by the employer were not fulfilled. You were led on at work for several years with the promised hope that things would improve.

The employer probably feels that any promises that were made were based upon his or her definition of when the economy would "pick up." To the employer, the economy may not have picked up sufficiently to warrant restoration of pay. In fact, one of the reasons for the cut in pay was perhaps to provide sufficient funds to remodel the building.

Also, the employer may argue that the Employee Handbook limits promises that the employer can make. Many handbooks state that unless promises regarding pay or other changes of employment are made in writing and signed by the president, they are not enforceable. They would also argue that if you are "at-will" employees, subject to termination at the whim of the employer, then, likewise, your pay can be adjusted at the employer's discretion.

Simply being salaried workers does not make you exempt from overtime. Extra work performed on Saturdays to learn how to operate the new computers would not entitle you to extra overtime compensation if you are truly "exempt." Even though being salaried is one of the factors of being exempt, it is not the only one or even the most important one. Many employers incorrectly classify employees as exempt because they are salaried when the employees are really non-exempt and subject to overtime.

I would not suggest quitting unless you have another job available. But as a practical matter, there are several things that you can do. You could complain to the owner yourself, but this would carry the risk of being branded a troublemaker. You could have a group of employees complain together to the employer without identifying you as the "leader of the pack." You could request the employer let you work a four-day week because your pay had been cut 20%. You could draft a respectful letter to the employer raising these issues as concerns, but not particularly as demands. If the promises are in writing and had further details, you would have a better case.

8

JOB TRAINING PROMISES

*Job Training Promise
Should Have Been Kept*

Q Recently I left a job to take another position. I told my new employer during an interview that I hadn't worked with their software for 15 years, and he told me that I would be fully trained. The woman that I replaced would come in on weekends to train me.

I started to work on Nov. 8 and received 2½ days of training on the computer. I was terminated Dec. 2.

Do I have any protection because he didn't live up to his agreement? I also found out after I took the job that the employer and the woman I replaced are living together.

—L.F., Mission Viejo

A Promises can be enforced. You can recover damages for any breach of a contract made with you. The problem is proving that they really promised to fully train you in your new job. If it was confirmed in writing or if you have a witness, you would have a stronger case. However, even if it is your word against another's, it still may be good enough.

There may be a conflict over the extent to which they were to train you. Since you feel that the training was entirely inadequate, it would help if you could get authorities in your industry to agree with you.

A large factor of any case is the extent of damages that are suffered.

If you could prove that the breach of contract was not just negligent, but intentional, then you could establish a fraud case. Fraud is breach of contract with intent and provides for a greater measure of damages. You can recover lost wages as well as "punitive" or punishment damages. There has been some doubt as to whether or not a fraud action will be legally permitted in an employment case. According to a recent court ruling, if the fraud occurred at the beginning of employment, then it can be an appropriate claim.

A large factor of any case is the extent of damages suffered as a result of the wrongful act of the employer. It appears you have given up a lot. You left a job to take this position. That gives your case more of an emotional impact to those evaluating it. If you got a better job soon after losing this old one, your case does not have as much potential as if it took you a long period of time to find a replacement job.

I do not see the relevance of your being trained by a woman whom you replaced and who was living with your boss. If the woman you replaced has reclaimed the job, then you might have a discrimination claim.

Even though you received a short period of training, they did not fire you until several weeks later. If the lack of training were not the reason for the termination, I would question the value of your case.

9

JOB-SITE CLOSING PROMISES

Firm Liable If It Made False Promises
To Close

Q We are employed by a major corporation that told us they were closing our location in May. With the encouragement of our manager, we went out and found other jobs. Now, they are saying they are not closing and will not give severance pay as promised.

Do we have any legal recourse?

—F.T., Fullerton

A Large corporations are required to give advance notice of at least 60 days to employees who may be subject to a layoff when a business location closes. An employer who fails to give such notice may have to pay two months' salary to these employees as a penalty. The intent is to provide the employees adequate notice to find other employment.

> *Large corporations are required to give advance notice of a layoff when a business location closes.*

Apparently, your employer gave you such notice. The problem is what they specifically promised. If they told you definitely that they were going to close that location by a certain date and promised certain severance along with it, you would have a very good case for breach of contract. If their promises said only that they might be closing in several months, then your rights would not be so definite.

If you have any information that the employer used this method to intentionally or fraudulently reduce the number of its employees rather than laying them off or firing them, you may be entitled not only to your actual severance benefits but "punitive" damages as well.

> *If your severance pay is less than $5,000, consider filing a small claims lawsuit.*

I suggest you evaluate how specific the employer really was. Send a letter detailing your claims. If your severance pay is less than $5,000, consider filing a small claims lawsuit against them. The California Labor Commissioner may be of some assistance as well.

Promises can be enforced.

WAGES

10

PAY CUTS

Cut in Pay Raises Legal Questions

Q Can an employee be forced into taking a pay cut that would effectively eliminate payment for over-time hours worked?

If so, shouldn't some written notice be required prior to enforcement of the rate reduction?

One day, the supervisor informed me of a new policy dealing with "inconvenience time."

Prior to implementing the new policy, my regular hourly rate was $9.63 and overtime was $19.26 per hour. The new policy lowered the hourly rate to $8.10 and included one hour of "inconvenience time"—paid at $12.15 per hour—each work day. This hour of "inconvenience time" is to be paid whether or not the hour of overtime is actually worked.

This new policy effectively eliminates payment for one hour of overtime each day. I will now have to work up to 99 hours for the same pay I was receiving for an 88-hour pay period. This new policy amounts to an average loss of $225 per month.

Do I have grounds for legal action since this pay reduction was not based on performance? If so, is there an agency I should contact?

—F.M., Irvine

A There is no law that prohibits decreasing an employee's pay if it does not violate promises to the employee in the past or minimum wage law.

However, if it can be shown that the pay reduction is simply a pretext to avoid paying overtime, then it may be illegal. An obvious example is when the pay cut applies only for a short period of time. If a retail business cuts your pay in the months before the busy time of Christmas and then restores it to the old level in January, it would be illegal. In fact, the shorter the duration of the pay cut, the more provable your case would be.

> *There is no law that prohibits decreasing an employee's pay if it does not violate promises to the employee in the past or minimum wage law.*

It might be more difficult to prove that a permanent pay cut is illegal. The California Labor Commissioner's office oversees wage and hour violations.

You may not be losing as much money as you think, however. Apparently, you were being paid overtime at twice your normal hourly rate. Employers are required to pay only 1½ times the hourly rate for work over 40 hours a week.

> *If a pay reduction is simply a pretext to avoid paying overtime, it may be illegal.*

Also, consider the advantages of receiving an hour of "inconvenience time" even if you do not work that extra hour. If your employer does not ask you to work too much overtime, you might end up making almost the same money per hour that you did before.

11

RETROACTIVE CUTBACKS

Retroactive Cutbacks in Pay
Against the Law

Q I received my last paycheck and my pay was decreased. When I asked my supervisor, he said cuts were being made to increase profits and that there was no other option if I wanted my job.

Doesn't my employer have to discuss pay cuts with me first? Is it illegal for them to do this?

—T.S., Fullerton

A It is illegal for an employer to cut your pay for work that you have already performed. If you complain about it, it is also illegal for an employer to retaliate by disciplining, demoting, or firing you.

There is usually nothing to prevent an employer from reducing your pay in the future. Pay cuts are sometimes the only way to decrease expenses and prevent layoffs.

If an employer has made promises regarding the duration of any pay amount, however, it is improper to change that commitment. Did your boss promise you that your former pay would last any set duration of time? Do you have a written employment agreement?

It is illegal for an employer to cut your pay for work you have already performed. If you complain about it, it is also illegal for them to retaliate against you.

An employer may also have an obligation to give "reasonable notice" of anticipated pay cuts. This is especially true if employees have worked for an extended period of time and have made financial commitments based upon assurances that they would continue to receive certain compensation.

It would certainly have been more diplomatic for your employer to have given you a reasonable amount of notice about this change. However, from the employer's point of view, too much notice might encourage employees to depart prematurely.

12

PAY COLLUSION

*It's Legal for Firms
to Get Together on Pay*

Q The firm I work for recently changed its pay policy so that base pay will be adjusted to be equivalent to similar jobs at other companies in our field, as
determined by annual surveys. Base pay will increase
only through promotions or changes in survey results.
All other increases are in the form of bonuses based
on the company meeting performance goals. In the
past, these goals have been met only by severe downsizing.

Supposedly, this survey method of compensation
soon will be the industry norm. My question is, if these
companies are all surveying each other to determine
employee compensation, which one would take the hit
on profitability first by raising salaries for, say, the
cost of living? Do employees have any protection
under the law from employer collusion under these
conditions?

—M.Y., Tustin

A Employers have a right to discuss levels of compensation with other employers and base their own compensation plan upon standards in the industry. In fact, the State of California regularly surveys unions and employers throughout the state to determine the prevailing wage that it sets for certain trades and crafts in the construction industry. Just as employers have a constitutional right of free speech, so do the employees through collective bargaining. Employers cannot retaliate against employees for pursuing these rights.

Consultation between employers becomes "collusion" only when the employers coordinate pay practices for unlawful violation of rules, such as overtime, minimum wage, right to associate and discuss union activities or equal opportunity in employment. You may have a claim against your employer if you can show that the violation of one of these laws is, at least in part, the result of such collusion. You should not confuse employers trying to coordinate lower salaries with employers illegally fixing the price of their goods for consumers.

Consultation between employers becomes improper "collusion" only when the employers coordinate pay practices for unlawful violation of rules.

Which employer will make the first move to increase salary depends upon their desire to retain valuable employees who might otherwise quit. This is really no different than many other businesses that must meet the "going rate."

Lastly, before you decide that your employer's system is improper, evaluate its possible advantages. Your salary increase is tied to certain performance goals and may be even more secure or give possibly higher raises than one linked to the cost of living.

13
COMMISSION CHANGES

*Firms Usually Can Reshape Their
Commission Policy*

Q I have been employed for eight years and my commission aside from my salary was 3% of gross
income. However, due to the slowdown in business,
they decided to restructure the commission. It had not
changed even last year until new management came
in. Do I have recourse legally since the commission
structure was the same for seven years? Are they acting in bad faith?

—W.L., La Palma

A An employer must abide by its promises to its
employees. The problem is the duration of the
promises. Most employers do not commit themselves

to a length of time during which any promises regarding wages or commissions will remain effective. They like to reserve the opportunity in the future, based on market conditions and other factors, to adjust compensation either up or down. Unless your employer gave you a definite promise that the commission program would last a certain amount of time, he or she probably has the right to change it.

An employer must abide by its promises to its employees. The problem is the duration of the promises.

However, any change to the commission program should not be made retroactively. Certainly any closed sales under the old plan should be paid according to that plan.

There is often a problem on sales that are "in progress." For example, if you have completed 95% of the work for closing the sale over an extended period of time, but the customer finally signs a contract after the employer announces a new commission plan, you have been unreasonably deprived of compensation you would otherwise have earned.

A fair employer will institute a new commission program for new sales or for a time period in the future.

A fair employer will institute a new commission program for new sales or for a time period in the future. If the employer initially reserved the right to "officially" change the commission program at will until after a sale is confirmed, then you would have to live with that understanding.

You may want to talk candidly with new management about easing in the new program for future sales only. Weigh the advantages of arguing your rights to current management with the disadvantages of any ill will that it may cause toward you.

14
RAISES

Just Take the Raise,
Whatever the Amount

Q Our employer is engaging in a salary administration practice that I'm not sure is legal. On March
2, our annual pay rate increase took effect. However,
we were not notified of what the new rate was until
several days later.

Shouldn't we be told what the new rate is before it
takes effect? How can our employer withhold this information for days when we're already working at the
new rate? I don't understand what would motivate
them to do this.

—S.H., La Habra

A An employer has an obligation to clearly tell employees the rate at which they are paid. In fact, it would be illegal if your employer told you that your salary is decreasing to a level that will be divulged later.

However, the opposite is not as true. When the employer tells you that your wage has increased and they will notify you later, it could be regarded as a discretionary bonus not subject to the same laws as if it had been a decrease. Even though

An employer has an obligation to tell employees the rate at which they are paid.

it would be nice to budget your own personal finances by knowing the increased amount, it is not unusual for employers to tell employees that they will be receiving a bonus or an increase in pay that will be made retroactive to an earlier date.

It might be different if the employer had an obligation to grant this increase, perhaps as part of a contract. However, if it is a discretionary raise in pay, the same legalities do not exist.

Also, you would have a better case if the delay in informing you was greater than just "several days." Any possible damage you would suffer because of this situa-

Your wage increase could be regarded as a discretionary bonus not subject to the same laws as if it had been a decrease.

tion is so minimal that you should probably ignore the inconvenience and be grateful for the increase. Even if they had an obligation to tell you, I would not suggest antagonizing the employer for the minor inconvenience it caused you.

15

BONUSES

Written Policy Needed to
Seek Unpaid Bonus

QAbout three years ago, I accepted a job with the understanding that the company's incentive bonus plan was part of my compensation, with a target bonus of 15%. This was clearly stated in their offer letter to me. The plan has a detailed formula for payout based on company and individual performance.

The company's performance and my performance were excellent, and I was paid the bonus for two years. I left the company four months ago at the end of the full financial year, but the company will not pay me the accrued bonus. The literature associated with the plan states that an employee must be employed for the full 12 months of the company's financial year (I was) to be eligible for payout and that the payout is to be made within 90 days from the end of the financial year.

I gave several weeks' notice and left for a new job after the end of the year. I got a beautiful crystal and plaque in recognition for my leadership and many kind words, but no bonus.

The brochure for the bonus plan states that the "official plan document" governs the administration of the plan. However, my letter and follow-up calls have only resulted in verbal comments that they don't plan to pay me and they are still looking for the "official plan document."

Do I go get a lawyer or is there a better way?

—D.B., Mission Viejo

❖   ❖   ❖

A Employers should comply with their promises. If you qualify for the incentive bonus plan according to the program, then you should be paid accordingly. The employer also is supposed to pay what they owe you upon termination.

The problem is that you do not have the "official plan document." I suggest that before you file a lawsuit or go to a lawyer, send another letter with a stronger threat of going to a lawyer unless the matter is resolved.

If you qualify for the incentive bonus plan according to the program, then you should be paid accordingly.

You might also consider asking some of your friends who are current employees of the company to obtain a copy of the document for you. The company may be more willing to cooperate with a current employee than a past employee. You can also speak directly to the administrator of the plan, if it is an outside party. You might get the official document easier that way.

If you still do not get results, consider either going to an attorney, who will then write a letter or file a lawsuit, or contact the California Labor Commissioner's office, which will assist you.

16

NON-COMMISSION WORK

He Dislikes Being Out of Commission

Q I am employed as a regular full-time "big ticket" sales associate at a national retailer. My compensation consists of 100% commission (no base) with payback draw.

My questions are:

1) Since I am a regular full-time sales associate and on 100% commission, can I be requested to leave the selling floor to complete non-selling tasks before completing 40 hours a week of pure selling time?

2) Since I am on 100% commission, can I be required to attend store meetings or training meetings without being reimbursed my average pay for time spent? I have been refused any pay for meetings under an hour; for those over an hour, I am paid $5 an hour.

—R.S., Mission Viejo

A Employers are required to pay employees a minimum wage. This is computed according to each paycheck. Your commission accrued during a particular pay period, after being divided by the total hours worked during that pay period, must exceed the minimum wage. If it does not, the employer is obligated to pay you the minimum wage for that pay period.

Whether or not you are performing non-commission tasks during a certain pay period is not really the issue. What you should be concerned about is whether or not you have earned the minimum wage. Your employer can agree to pay you whatever additional amount the company desires. If your employer has agreed to pay you $5 an hour for meetings that exceed one hour and that are unrelated to your commission, then the company is obligated to that commitment.

Problems arise when your commission income for a particular pay period exceeds the minimum wage but then might not for the next period. That is the reason why many employers give their sales people a minimum base, which gets around that problem.

Many employers assume, too, that salespeople will be doing a certain amount of non-commission work and training, even when they are paid on a commission basis. They believe that the commission more than makes up for other time that is simply part of the job. It is similar to comparing "piecework" systems, in which a person is paid according to the number of units produced or sold. Regardless of the method, minimum wages must be paid.

As a practical answer, you should evaluate whether the commission more than makes up for the "downtime" of your other duties and assignments. Rather than complaining about the pay period in which you did not make minimum wage and angering your superiors, you might want to keep track of it in writing and then bring it up later if you are laid off or fired or you quit.

The deadline for making such claims is usually two years. It is illegal for the company to retaliate against you—whether through demotion, failure to promote, layoff or termination—for making a wage complaint.

17

EXPENSE REIMBURSEMENT

Employer Must Pick Up Job-Related Expenses

Q We have a family member who has been in a clerical position for two years. Recently the company
was turned over to new management and the employee was told that he must travel to an eastern city,
secure hotel accommodations at his expense, and
attend a weeklong seminar in order to ensure continued employment. Is that legal?

—J.T., Fullerton

An employer must reimburse employees for all of the expenses incurred through employment pursuant to Labor Code 2902. This includes the cost of travel and hotel accommodations. It is a common practice for employees to pay various expenses and be reimbursed for them later. If it is a great hardship on the employee to cover the costs, an employer might have to pay the costs initially.

An employer must reimburse employees for all of the expenses incurred through employment. This includes the cost of travel and hotel accommodations.

It is unclear why a clerical worker would be required to go to a weeklong seminar. It may be reasonable if the purpose is to train for new duties or to be informed of revised policies of the new management.

Also, determine if the company treated other employees differently, and if so, why. It is illegal if the difference in treatment is based on discrimination or improper retaliation.

Your family member might want to suggest in a very diplomatic letter that management consider having the seminar here if it is simply to educate current employees. Also explain to them the problems in paying the cost of the travel or accommodations. Ask them to either pay it initially or promptly reimburse it.

18
EMPLOYER LOSSES

Employees Can't Be Held Liable for Employer Loss

Q At the restaurant where I work as a waitress, I carry around cash and make change for the customers. At the end of the evening, I give the amount of each check to the restaurant. What are the rules governing this? Twice, I've had to make up the difference when a customer has walked out without paying. Am I legally obligated to pay the difference?

—L., Huntington Beach

A Generally, an employee can't be responsible for employer losses. In fact, if they fire you because you refuse to make up the difference, you may have a claim against them for wrongful termination of your employment.

In a recent court case similar to your situation, a salesman sold an item, the customer paid the purchase price, and a commission was paid. Thereafter, the item was found to be defective and the customer returned it for credit. The company subtracted the commission already paid from the salesman's next salary check. The court decided that this practice was illegal. Once the customer paid the bill, the commission was earned. The fact that the sale item was defective was not the fault of the salesman. The employer was forced to shoulder its own losses.

> *You should complain in writing about the problem so you can document your efforts to get the employer to follow the law.*

Your restaurant may justify this policy to prevent waitresses from diverting the money paid to their own use. Even though the restaurant cannot dock you for lost money, if they question your honesty, they do have the right to fire you or impose other disciplinary actions.

As a practical matter, I would suggest that whenever a customer fails to pay the check, you immediately inform your manager to prevent suspicion at the end of the day. If you complain about the practice or refuse to abide by it and they fire you, they may deny their policy or your prior complaints. Therefore, you should complain in writing about the problem so you can document your efforts to get the employer to follow the law.

19

CAR COSTS

Expenses Have to Be Repaid

Q My question concerns driving on the job and being paid 29 cents a mile. Should insurance costs be covered by the employee or the employer?

—J.M., Atwood

A Employers are required by law to reimburse employees for expenses such as the cost of driving. If 29 cents a mile covers the actual cost to you for mileage, maintenance and insurance, then the employer has fulfilled it obligations to you. It is your burden to show to the employer that your total cost of driving, including insurance, exceeds the per-mile charge that the employer has allocated to it.

As a practical matter, if you are asking for more reimbursement than the company has allocated for its employees, you may get your past costs paid but harm future employment. If you are driving, for example, a Rolls-Royce as a pizza delivery car and your employer does not want to pay future estimated high insurance costs, you can be terminated. [The 1998 standard rate is 32.5 cents.]

PAYCHECKS

20

TIMELY

PAY

Law Doesn't Permit Stalling on Paychecks

Q For two years, I have been working for a small manufacturing company as a sales and marketing manager. Since then, sales have steadily increased due to the new markets I chose to explore. Last year I successfully negotiated a 20% increase in my base pay along with a higher commission rate.

Although my base pay is paid bimonthly as agreed, my commission checks are consistently late, sometimes by two months. I am constantly forced to remind the owner to pay me as scheduled. Because of the company's size, I have no one else to complain to.

Is there a legal time frame in which I should be issued a commission check? Under my original agreement, it was to be paid on the 20th day after the month's end. Also, is my employer required to disclose figures from which he is calculating commissions?

—R.T., Long Beach

A California State Law requires the prompt payment of wages. Even though commission compensation is to be paid "when earned," the question is the date it was earned. In the past, the employer was supposed to pay you on the 20th day after month's end. Unless the employer committed to the payment date for a defined period of time, there is nothing to prevent him from subsequently changing the payment date.

Even though commission compensation is to be paid "when earned," the question is the date it was earned.

Some employers say that a commission is earned once an order is submitted. Others may require receipt of the money from the customer before a commission is earned. Once the event giving you the right to the commission is fulfilled, the date of payment is the next issue. You receive the base salary bimonthly, but the commission does not necessarily have to be paid in a similar manner.

You might remind your employer, in writing, of the original commitment on when the commission is to be paid. You might also request in writing the figures for calculating the commissions.

It is illegal for an employer to retaliate against an employee for complaining about wages that are due and payable. If the employer has agreed to pay the commissions by a certain date and retaliates against you for its failure to pay, it could be liable for damages to you.

If you discover inaccurate figures were used for your commissions, you might have a claim for fraud. Make sure you have as much documentation as possible on the commissions you are owed in case you are suddenly fired for complaining.

21

BOUNCED PAYCHECKS

Workers' Paychecks Late, Bounce

Q We are paid twice a month, about the 15th and the last day of the month. On Jan. 13 and on Feb. 28, our paychecks bounced. After that, we demanded cashier's checks from our employer because of the hassle of going to the employer's bank, verifying sufficient funds, cashing the paychecks and then going to our own bank to make deposits.

Since then, our pay has been late four times. We suspect our employer has discovered "free" money and/or is a total control freak, because our sales have been excellent. Throughout this, we have endured fees for depositing bad checks, extra interest, credit dings and other turmoil.

Our most recent pay period was the last straw. The pay was nine calendar days late and drawn on regular checks. We filed a complaint with the labor board, which allegedly will investigate and levy a stiff fine. But what about restitution for the employees? We are floating the idea of taking one hour of overtime pay or compensatory time off for each day a check is late or bounces. Is there any legal redress?

—J.M., Atwood

A It is a criminal violation for any employer to fail to pay employees in a timely manner at least twice a month or to bounce paychecks.

Whether you go to the Labor Commissioner or directly to the district attorney's office, the result is the same—criminal prosecution. It may end up in possible fines that go to the State of California or imprisonment. In any event, it does not result in money going into your pocket unless there is still compensation owed to you.

Compliance with the Labor Code is presumed to be part of every employment contract. If your employer fails to comply with these rules, technically he is in breach of his contract with you. You accordingly could have a claim against him for breach of contract.

Additionally, if the employer retaliates against you in any way by laying you off or firing you because of your complaints about their unlawful practices, you would have an additional "tort" claim of wrongful termination or retaliation. Through this type of claim, you might not only recover your out-of-pocket damages, but also punitive (punishment) damages as well.

If you want to make a move to another employer, you may want to document your complaints to your current employer and wait for the retaliation to come. If you can document the linkage between your complaints and their retaliation against you by reducing your work, changing your assignment, laying you off or firing you, you would have a viable tort claim.

According to the Labor Code, an employer must reimburse an employee for business expenses, which may include expenses incurred for bounced checks.

There is another procedure that allows you to recover three times the amount of a bounced check up to $500 if the writer of a check fails to pay you the amount of the bounced check within 30 days of your sending them a certified notice of their violation.

The last option is to simply quit and seek employment with a more reputable employer.

22

BANKRUPTCY AND PAY PRIORITY

Bankruptcy No Excuse for
Withholding Pay

Q I was recently terminated after my employer filed for Chapter 11 bankruptcy reorganization.

Approximately 40% of the work force was terminated in the middle of a pay period. When everyone was let go, there was no severance, earned or accrued vacation, or regular pay for time worked. The human resources manager told everyone that they would have to petition the courts to receive anything. After challenging the manager's statements, one worker was told, "So sue us."

My personal dilemma is that I had a severance agreement, signed by the chief financial officer, that included eight weeks' earned and accrued vacation, plus four months' salary. When I left, I was told that the agreement and my last two weeks' salary would be turned over to the courts.

I have contacted a number of state and federal agencies, as well as an attorney, and I have been told that state labor officials, the federal Equal Employment Opportunity Commission, or any other state or federal agency cannot assist in recovering what is due me.

Is there anyone out there that supports the "little

people" against corporations that trash their employ-ees? I was with this company for 14 years.

—G.P., Westminster

❖   ❖   ❖

A Your claim does not disappear simply because your employer filed for bankruptcy. It means that you need to get in line with other creditors.

Your claim for wages of up to $2,000 will be given priority over general creditors if the money was earned during the 90 days before the bankruptcy was filed. But a claim for severance or wages exceeding $2,000 would be grouped with claims of other creditors. This prioritizing determines who gets paid first from the available money of the corporation. It also might affect what percentage of your claim is ultimately paid and the timing of it.

Your claim does not disappear because your employer filed for bankruptcy.

It is surprising that you were told the State Labor Commissioner could not help you. They have handled such claims in the past.

But you have other options. You could file a claim with the bankruptcy court yourself. You should have been named as a creditor and received certain documents to make a claim. It is not too difficult to fill them out and send them in.

Also, consider a fraud action against the officers of the corporation. It has a legal obligation to pay employees on time. Officers also may face a personal liability if they lied to you about wages that should have been paid. Conceivably, you might recover your lost wages plus additional sums to compensate you for your distress over the situation and to punish officers for any wrongdoing.

23

PAY

SCHEDULE

Monthly Paycheck
Appears to Be Illegal

Q I recently started a new position at a company with about eight employees. My employer pays a monthly salary.

A friend told me that only government workers could be paid monthly; everyone else must be paid weekly or bimonthly.

—T.C., Santa Monica

A From what you say, your employer is in violation of law. The general rule is that employees must be paid twice a month.

Exceptions to this rule include automobile salespeople, who can be paid once per month on their commissions, and state government workers.

It also is illegal for your employer to retaliate against you if you complain about it. I would suggest writing an informal note to raise the issue, and keeping a copy of it.

24

DIRECT DEPOSIT

Cancel Direct Deposit if Cash Needed on Payday

Q I'm signed up for direct deposit with my employer. Payday is Tuesday, but they claim they cannot release the funds until 12:01 a.m. Wednesday. Are they obligated to make my pay available on payday?

—C.P., Los Angeles

A Employers must pay wages within 10 days of the payroll period. The employer will no doubt argue that direct deposit is an accommodation for you. And if you ask to be paid with a check that you deposit at your bank, you might not be able to get the funds released until it clears your bank the next day.

If this is an important issue to you, you can terminate the direct deposit method and cash your payroll check at the employer's bank on payday. You also could change your bank to the employer's bank so that you would receive immediate credit for the check.

It is illegal for an employer to retaliate against an employee for complaining about wages that are due and payable.

OVERTIME

25

OVERTIME DEADLINES

Worker With Unpaid Overtime Should Get Lawyer

Q I was once a non-exempt employee who, despite my requests, was not paid for overtime work performed from January through March of 1990. My employer even has a written policy, dated in February, 1991, providing for such overtime. I am being laid off in about three months and would like to know if I can again request the overtime pay I was denied in early 1990. Can I obtain copies of the time sheets that I submitted to our human resources department showing the overtime hours for this period?

—F.C., Irvine

A There is no doubt that you should have been paid your overtime compensation. The problem is that you have passed most of the statute of limitations deadlines for filing your claim. The deadline for breach of oral contract is two years, breach of a statutory duty requiring overtime compensation is three years, and breach of a written contract is four years from the date of the breach. It appears that you have passed all of these deadlines based on your employer's failure to pay in early 1990.

However, you still might have a valid claim based upon the company's written policy dated February, 1991. By putting the policy in writing, the company then created a new four-year deadline from that date to reclaim the unpaid wages. Since your personal attempts to resolve your action have not succeeded, your only recourse would be to go to an attorney.

California state law requires that the employer allow you to look at all relevant documents in your employee file and obtain a copy of any document that you signed. Put your request in writing to confirm that you made the request. The employer can be subject to liability if it fails to comply.

> *The deadline for breach of oral contract is two years, breach of a statutory duty requiring overtime compensation is three years, and breach of a written contract is four years from the date of the breach.*

26
SALARY AND OVERTIME

Even Salaried Workers Can Get Overtime Pay

Q Recently, I was changed from salaried to hourly status. I was told this was in the interest of "uniformity." My pay rate was reduced when calculated on an hourly basis, but my employer said I could make it up by being paid for overtime.

This development has hurt my morale. Several coworkers and I are in the same boat. I would appreciate your ideas on this.

—P.O., Whittier

A This move by your employer makes me wonder whether you might have been entitled to overtime while you were salaried. One of the biggest misconceptions in the workplace is that being salaried eliminates any overtime claims.

It does not matter what your job title was or what the employer called you. What matters is your actual job assignment. There is a very good chance that the employer might owe you overtime compensation for the last three years—the statute of limitations for claiming overtime—if your duties haven't changed.

> One of the biggest misconceptions in the workplace is that being salaried eliminates any overtime claims.

If your employer reduced the compensation of all employees, whether they were salaried or not, then the action may be legitimate. However, simply lowering the compensation of those who are now being allowed to receive overtime pay appears to be illegal. If you complain about it, it is also illegal for your employer to fire you or otherwise retaliate against you.

But you face a practical dilemma. Even though the law is on your side, if you complain, there is a good chance that you may alienate your boss, particularly if you also claim overtime for the last three years.

> Every day you wait to pursue your rights, you are waiving a possible claim of overtime from three years ago.

Remember, however, that every day you wait to pursue your rights, you are waiving a possible claim of overtime from three years ago.

27
OVERTIME RECOURSE

*Which Government Agency For
Whistleblowers or Wage Claims?*

Q I am confused. Do the state and federal govern-
ments have different rules for overtime pay? If I
have an overtime claim, should I go to the state Labor
Commissioner or to the federal Department of Labor?

—M.S., Newport Beach

A Overtime regulations are the most common laws broken by employers. Not only are there different state and federal laws, but there are scores of exceptions to the rules—and exceptions to the exceptions. No wonder there is such confusion among both employers and employees.

It does make a difference whether a person evaluates an overtime claim by federal or state law. It also matters which of the agencies pursues a claim. For example, according to state regulations, a person can be exempt from overtime rules even if their compensation is on a non-salaried basis. This is usually not the case under federal rules. If a person is not on salary, overtime rules usually apply. Of course, there are exceptions depending upon the nature of the work. The point is, filing a claim with one agency might result in success while filing with the other might mean failure.

Overtime regulations are the most common laws broken by employers.

If a person is not on salary, overtime rules usually apply.

As a practical solution, I suggest going to either of the two agencies until they accept your claim. The problem is they may accept your claim but not pursue it for all of the benefits to which you may be entitled. I recently met with a person who filed certain claims with the state agency. After we reviewed the case, we discovered that tens of thousands of dollars worth of other claims had been overlooked. The most reliable method of knowing which agency to use or which laws most fully benefit you is to consult an attorney with experience in this area of the law.

28
SALARIED/
EXEMPT STATUS

Salaried and Exempt Aren't Identical

Q What is the law concerning salaried, exempt employees? My company is currently on a seven-hours-a-day, 35-hour workweek. In October, we will begin working eight hours a day, 40 hours a week and the company does not plan to increase our pay, so we'll be working an extra five hours at the same salary. Is that legal?

—T.D., La Habra

A The increase of work hours to eight hours per day, 40 hours per week does not violate any wage-and-hour laws. If an employee is on a salaried basis, employment hours can vary at the option of the employer. Simply being salaried does not mean that an employee is also exempt. This is a very common misconception in the workplace.

Often the only recourse for an exempt employee who is asked to work unreasonably lengthy hours may be to quit.

A non-exempt employee will enjoy the protection of many laws that require rest breaks, lunch breaks and a limitation in duration of employment hours. An employee may have possible rights in this situation if previous promises by the employer have been made regarding the permanency of the work-hour policy, or if the change unlawfully discriminates or retaliates against one particular group of employees.

Unfortunately, often the only recourse for an exempt employee who is asked to work unreasonably lengthy hours may be to quit. The salaried, non-exempt worker at least has a right to overtime pay.

29

EXEMPT STATUS

Companies Can Ask Plenty of Their Exempt Employees

Q I recently accepted a senior management position with a small commercial bank. After starting work I have learned of the following personnel practices:

1. The probationary period for nonexempt employees is 90 days, while it is six months for exempt employees. Probationary employees are not paid for holidays that occur during their probationary period.

2. Exempt employees are required to record their daily starting and ending times, as well as lunch periods, in a log and are required to work at least eight hours per day.

3. All employees are expected to work at least two Saturdays a month. While nonexempt employees receive overtime pay, the exempt employees receive neither overtime nor compensating time off.

4. Various employees are, on occasion, required to drive among the three branches during the day but are not reimbursed for the mileage expense.

The bank's personnel policy discloses the probationary period but does not mention the other practices. Are these practices legal?

—J.B., Fullerton

A Apparently you learned of these workplace problems after you started working for your employer. The answers to your questions:

1. An employer is entitled to define the probationary period for each class of employee. Employers are not required to compensate any employees for holiday pay. If, however, the employer promises to pay for holidays, probationary employees can be excluded from that benefit.

2. Federal rules require that exempt workers be paid on a salary basis. Specifying starting and ending times is inconsistent with exempt status.

If employers do not treat an exempt worker as they should, that exempt status will be lost.

There is certainly nothing wrong with requiring that employees record their hours worked for billing purposes, however. It also is proper for an employer to require exempt employees to specify times when they are in the office so an employer knows their whereabouts.

An employer can require exempt employees to work eight hours per day. However, employees can't be "docked" if they don't work the minimum amount of time. The employer can only fire these employees or put them on an hourly basis.

If employers do not treat an exempt worker as they should, that exempt status will be lost. Once that status changes from exempt to nonexempt, the employee will qualify for a host of additional protections, including overtime compensation.

3. There is nothing illegal about an employee requiring exempt workers to work two Saturdays per month. There is no doubt that employers can take advantage of exempt workers.

4. Employees must be reimbursed for their expenses related to work.

A non-exempt employee will enjoy the protection of many laws that require rest breaks, lunch breaks and a limitation in duration of employment hours.

TIME CARDS

30

CLOCK-IN
LAWS

Time Really Counts For Clock-In Workers

Q The company I work for has just started a new policy. It states that any employee who forgets to clock in or out has 15 minutes automatically deducted. And if you punch in even one minute late, you are also docked 15 minutes. Yet you are expected to start working right away.

This is true whether you punch in one minute or 14 minutes late. The company pays only in 15-minute increments. Is this legal? Can a company make up these kinds of policies? It seems that if you work an extra 10 minutes and are paid hourly, you should be paid for this time.

—L.D., Huntington Beach

A An employer is required to pay you for all work performed. According to federal law, an employer can round off your time as long as it averages out to be the appropriate amount of time that should have been paid to you anyway. This means, however, that your time could either go back to the time that you should have started or forward to the next established increment, whether it be to the tenth of an hour or to the quarter of an hour.

An employer is required to pay you for all work performed.

It does not appear that your employer is following this law. The company actually is making money off your lateness. Even if you are one minute late, it doesn't pay you until the next 15 minutes. They improperly round it off ahead but not back.

There is a state law that states that if an employee arrives at work late, with a loss of time less than 30 minutes, an employer can deduct half an hour's wage. This appears to be in the nature of a penalty. If there is any conflict between different laws, the California Labor Commissioner's office will enforce the more favorable law for the employee. According to the Labor Commissioner's office, the federal law requiring payment for all time worked should prevail over this state statute.

It is illegal to retaliate against you if you complain about a violation of these rules.

It is illegal for your employer to retaliate against you if you complain about a violation of these rules. If you think that complaining will brand you as a troublemaker, simply keep track of the time for which you have not been paid and make a claim if and when you are fired or laid off.

31

DENIED BREAKS

Numerous Potential Claims for Denied Breaks

Q I worked for a large company and was denied breaks for two years. I was wondering if it was too late to seek compensation, as it has been two to three years since I worked there.

—L.C., Aliso Viejo

A According to state law, an employer must provide a paid rest period of at least 10 minutes for non-exempt employees working at least 3½ hours in one day. For an eight-hour work period, two rest periods are required (in addition to an unpaid lunch break of at least 30 minutes). The required rest period must be, if possible, within the middle of the work period. It is clearly improper for your employer to deny you the breaks allowed you by law. You have a variety of ways to handle this matter.

If you rely upon breach of the statutory law, you have no additional claim for compensation because you were in fact paid for the time worked. You cannot treat the denied breaks as a claim for unpaid vacation. They do say, however, that complaints made to their office can result in a civil penalty against the employer payable to the state as well as an order to cease such practices in the future. The statute of limitations deadline for breach of a statute is three years from the date of each denial of breaks, which you still may be within.

You may also have contractual claims. If the employer orally represented that you would be allowed these breaks, then the deadline is two years from the date of each breach of such agreement, which you have passed. The deadline for breach of a written agreement is four years from the date of each breach. Thus, you still may have a claim in this regard.

If your employment ended because you complained about such practices, then you may also have a claim for illegal retaliation, with a three-year deadline from the date of your termination.

If you quit because you objected to the denial of your breaks, you might have a "constructive wrongful termination" case. You would have to show that the conditions of working there under those circumstances were so intolerable that any reasonable person would have likewise quit. This may have a three-year statute of limitations deadline from the date of termination.

Even if you do make a claim for compensation, evaluate whether it is even worth it. If it has been, for example 2½ years from the date of your termination, then you can realistically argue for a half year of denied breaks, at least on a statutory deadline of three years. Six months of denied breaks of 20 minutes per day would amount to approximately 43 hours at your normal hourly rate. Conceivably, if you show that the breaks would have extended a normal eight-hour work day to beyond that period, you might be able to argue overtime compensation of 1½ times your normal rate. Combining your claim for unpaid compensation with other potential claims might give your case enough substance to get your former employer's attention.

32
ON-DUTY PAY

Paid On-Duty Lunch Breaks OK

Q I work in a skilled nursing facility on the 11-7 shift and am the only licensed nurse on duty. The regulatory board for skilled nursing facilities states there must be a licensed nurse on duty 24 hours a day.

I am required to "clock out" for half an hour to satisfy the labor code for mealtime. I stay in the building and am available for emergencies. However, I am concerned about my liability should a legal problem arise while I'm "off the clock" and could not prove I responded to an emergency.

As I see it, I'm breaking the law and not complying with the 24-hour-a-day licensed nurse rule. Also, the labor code insists workers be relieved of their duties while off the clock. What do you advise about this situation?

—J.E., Newport Beach

A You should be concerned. Anything that might affect your license or personal liability must be addressed.

You might want to call the regulatory board overseeing the nursing facility and simply ask them about the "on-duty" requirements. It may be that they are more concerned that an actual nurse be responsible for the patients regardless of any violation of wage and hour rules.

Even though your employer may be violating the "clocking out" rules, they still may be in compliance with the on-duty rules if you, in fact, are fulfilling those responsibilities. Does the employer require you to stay in the building and be available for emergencies during your lunch break, or is that simply your own decision?

Your claim for compensation during your lunch break would be even more justifiable if the employer requires you to continue responsibilities during that time. Evaluate how often your break has been interrupted. Are you able to postpone non-emergency requests for help until after your break? The more your break is interrupted by emergencies, the better your argument will be.

An employer can actually have an employee remain on duty during their meal period if they are paid for that time and if the employer can show the necessity for it.

According to California law, an employer can actually have an employee remain on duty during their meal period if they are paid for that time and if the employer can show the necessity for it. There is not an absolute requirement, especially in the medical field, that an employee be allowed to leave the facilities during a lunch break. The key is that you need to be compensated for your time if you are on duty. It appears that paying you for your meal break is the most reasonable thing for the employer to do. It would certainly be very burdensome for them to have another nurse replace you for the half-hour meal period.

Consider informing the employer of their requirement to pay you for your lunch break so that you can remain technically "on duty." If they fire you for complaining about failure to pay you legally required compensation, you would have wrongful termination rights against them.

33

LUNCH MEETINGS

Mandatory Meetings at Lunch
Might Merit Pay

Q I work as a salaried employee in an office with a mix of salaried and hourly workers.

Due to a recent reorganization in the office we find ourselves with a temporary office manager who has decided that we should attend lunch meetings two or three times a week to improve communications and get better organized. We also have to attend scheduling, marketing and other organizational meetings as well.

Does an employer have the right to require employees to attend lunch meetings? Are the rules different for hourly employees?

—B.M., Canoga Park

A Employees who are exempt from overtime and various other workplace rules can be required to attend such meetings.

Simply being "salaried" does not necessarily make you exempt, however. You must also be classified and actually doing work as a professional (doctor, lawyer, etc.), manager (supervising two or more people more than half your time) or administrator.

Regardless of how your employer lists you, look at what you do to determine whether you are being properly classified as an exempt employee.

Regardless of how your employer lists you, look at what you do to determine whether you are being properly classified as an exempt employee.

If you are nonexempt, there are many additional rules regarding lunch and other breaks as well as overtime. Nonexempt workers can't be required to attend such meetings without appropriate compensation—their normal wage.

It would also be illegal for an employer to retaliate against an employee who complains about rule violations.

34

FORCED
TIME OFF

Time Off Should Be Taken Voluntarily

Q Some of my co-workers and I work for a company as exempt employees. At the time we were hired, we were told we would be paid a monthly salary plus benefits. But when a company project does not consume all of our time, we are told to either take time off without pay or use our vacation time to fill in the week.

It does not seem fair to ask employees to use their vacation benefits for the employer's benefit. As salaried employees, are we entitled to our salary from the company whether or not the project managers allow us to charge our time to their projects?

—G.W., Duarte

A An employer cannot force exempt workers to take time off without pay or use vacation time when it makes them leave early on any given day. You should be paid for the entire day, even if you worked part of it.

The employer will argue that if he has the power to fire you at will, he can also force you to take these leaves without pay.

As long as you are not fired or formally placed on an hourly basis, you deserve to be paid the full promised amount.

You could argue that as long as you are not fired or formally placed on an hourly basis, you deserve to be paid the full promised amount. Some court cases have held that the employer needs to pay workers for the balance of a pay period even if they have missed several days at the company's direction.

If your boss wants you to be essentially "on call" during your forced leave, your position is even stronger for your claim for compensation.

Combining your claim for unpaid compensation with one of your other potential claims might give your case enough substance to get your former employer's attention.

BENEFITS

35

HOLIDAY PAY

Firms Can Ban Holiday Work, Require Makeup Time

Q My husband works for a large company that makes its employees make up the time they take off for national holidays. Workers don't get the choice of working the holiday either. How cheap can a company get? Have you heard this before?

—R.L., Los Alamitos

A Companies are allowed to prohibit work on a national holiday, to pay compensation for the holiday and to require employees to make up the time later. They are restricted, however, as to how the work is to be made up.

The employer cannot require a non-exempt employee to work more than 40 hours in any week, along with other requirements, without paying appropriate overtime compensation.

Exempt employees have flexibility in work schedules to meet productivity requirements of the employer. But there is a risk that the exempt status may be destroyed if an employer requires an exempt employee to make up a day's missed time on another day or to give credit on one day for excess time worked on another. If that happens, the employer might have to comply with all of the rules for non-exempt status, including premium payment for overtime.

If an employee is not able to make up the time on a Saturday or a Sunday because of religious beliefs or family care commitments, the employer must reasonably accommodate such concerns to avoid legal liability.

If an employee is not able to make up the time on a Saturday or a Sunday because of religious beliefs or family care commitments, the employer must accommodate such concerns to avoid legal liability.

36
HOLIDAY POLICY

Holiday Policy Is Set By Employer

Q Since my company's customers are retail, we are often open on holidays that other office workers get off. On these slow days, such as the Fourth of July and the day after Thanksgiving, my department manager tells us that only one employee needs to come in. Everyone else is to take the day off as a vacation day.

With Christmas coming up, it doesn't seem fair that we will have to take the day before Christmas as a vacation day if we are willing to work it. Either the day is an office holiday or it's not.

Please advise if my company is violating the law.

—R.P., Los Alamitos

A There is no law that requires employers to honor any day as a holiday or even pay wages to employees who get holidays off. Even though this does not sound like the appropriate holiday spirit, the law is the law.

Employers, however, must abide by any promises made to employees regarding holiday time off or payment of wages for holidays. Additionally, employers can't enforce their holiday policy in a discriminatory manner.

In your situation, you probably won't complain too much if the one employee required to come in on those holidays is not you. But if you have to work holidays, evaluate if the policy is being applied unfairly. If each employee takes a turn, then it may be a fair policy. If the employer defines "office holiday" in its procedures handbook or oral policy as a paid day off for everyone except one employee on a rotating basis, then that is office policy. The challenge you have is to get a clear statement from the employer as to the precise policy.

There is no law that requires employers to honor any day as a holiday or even pay wages to employees who get holidays off.

If the employer promised that all of the employees would get certain holidays off and that these are paid holidays, you should be paid your actual time as well as the holiday pay.

I hate to be the bearer of bad news, but some employers can even change past favorable holiday policies, although they may have to give you sufficient warning of such change.

In any event, if the policy seems unfair, talk to your employer. Even the Grinch eventually changed his attitude.

37

VACATION ACCRUAL

Vacation-Time Policies are Not Set in Stone

Q If you're working for a company that contracts out for warehouse workers and then a new company takes over, does the new company still have to honor the contract regarding the amount of vacation time? I was promised four weeks of vacation after being there 13 years. But the new company says I have to start off at the bottom with one week of vacation. What is the legality of that?

—D.S., Yorba Linda

A There is no law that says that a company cannot change its compensation or benefit plan to its employees. Most "promises" of a company regarding wage rates or vacation policies are simply guidelines with no real definite duration commitment to them.

Of course, if you have a definite contract where wages or benefits are promised for a certain period of time, then you could claim that it is enforceable against the company for that length of time.

To the extent, however, that a company changes its policy, it still needs to compensate its employees to the extent benefits have accrued as of the date of such change. Thus, compensation would need to be paid for any wages or commissions that are payable as of the date of the change of policy. Likewise, employees are owed their accrued vacation up to the date of the change of policy.

One of the most confusing and often-violated employment practices concerns accrual of vacation time. If an employee is entitled to receive, for example, one week paid vacation after one year and two weeks after two years and the employment is terminated after a year and a half, he or she would be entitled to receive not only the one paid week accrued after the first anniversary, but also half of the two weeks that would have been accrued at the end of two years.

A company needs to compensate its employees for benefits accrued.

Many employers would wrongfully try to claim that the employee is not entitled to any further vacation until the employment passes the second-year mark. A successor company that has bought the stock or the assets of the original employer may be liable to the employees to the same extent. Purchase of one share or all the shares of stock of the original employer does not change the identity of the actual corporate employer.

The real issue arises when the change of ownership does not involve a stock purchase but rather an asset purchase of one degree or another. A recent case has held a successor company liable for the commissions and accrued benefits owed by the original company to its employees. The more assets bought by the successor company, the greater its responsibility will be to assume the accrued obligations of the original company.

38

VACATION PAY DUE ON LAYOFF

Many Avenues Can Be Taken in Dispute over Layoff

Q I worked for a publishing company until last spring, when I got into an argument with my supervisor. Two weeks later, I was conveniently "laid off" as part of a restructuring that eliminated my job only. On the day I was let go, I was given only four hours to clean out my desk.

All full-time employees at that company are given 10 hours each month to be used for vacations and sick leave. When I left the company, I was owed 45 such hours for which I have never been paid. Is there any way, short of a lawsuit, that I can get the company to give me the money due me?

—F.A., Dana Point

A The Labor Code requires payment of all wages upon discharge. "Wages" include accrued vacation time. Sick leave is not generally treated as "wages" by law, but if your employer had a policy that unpaid sick leave is payable upon termination of employment, then it too would be included as wages.

If the employer does not pay your wages as required, the wages for which it is responsible continue for up to 30 working days.

You may have other claims as well. Many companies have an "open door" policy and encourage dialogue to resolve differences. Your manager may have violated this policy if he was unnecessarily belligerent and vengeful, and you were laid off in bad faith. You may then have a claim for lost earnings until you find new work at equal pay.

"Restructuring" or "downsizing" is a legitimate reason for layoff, but it cannot be used as an excuse for violating company policies, discrimination or getting rid of whistle-blowers. If the "argument" you had with your employer concerned your objection to illegal practices or discrimination, and the employer retaliated against you for those objections, you would have a claim not just for lost wages, but also for emotional distress and even "punishment" damages.

Without filing a lawsuit through an attorney you can encourage your employer to pay you those wages in the following ways:

1. Explaining the law—Perhaps the easiest way to educate your former employers regarding the law is by sending them a copy of this response.

2. Labor Commissioner—The California Labor Commissioner will help you recover wage claims without charge.

3. Small-claims court—A quick alternative is filing a small-claims suit yourself. However, you are limited to $5,000, and if you win your employer can appeal it to a higher court, where attorneys would be used.

4. Attorney negotiation—Even without filing a suit, an attorney can put pressure on your employer to pay you what is owed.

39

VACATION DELAYS

No Specific Law on Vacation Request Delays

Q I work at a university in Los Angeles. When we request a vacation, we don't hear anything for months despite repeated inquiries. This makes it hard to get reservations and otherwise plan trips.

Shouldn't my boss be required to have some dead-line for responding to these requests, rather than sitting on them for four or five months? He also will take vacation requests from some co-workers months before the time requested, but rejects these requests from others. Some are told that they have to wait until the month of the date requested.

—R.S., Santa Clarita

A There is no law that requires any employer to grant paid or even unpaid vacations.

As a practical matter, however, most businesses have a vacation policy. If such policy exists, an employer must enforce it on an equal, non-discriminatory basis.

To accommodate their own work schedule, some employers simply close down for a period of time each year and require every employee to take their vacation at that specific time.

> *Most businesses have a vacation policy. If such policy exists, an employer must enforce it on an equal, non-discriminatory basis.*

Since you said that some but not all appear to get a runaround, you should question whether the employer's action discriminates against a certain group of people based on their age, race, sex or other relevant classification.

Evaluate the reasons for the double standards. Their practice might be illegal if it is discriminatory or is in retaliation for some whistle-blower action by those employees.

If the employer has a policy allowing employees to select their vacation months in advance, it might be held responsible if it does not allow you to do the same without reasonable justification.

40

TUITION REIMBURSEMENT

Tuition Reimbursement Not Guaranteed for All

Q My company has a tuition reimbursement program and guidelines stating that employees will be reimbursed for courses that have a direct relationship to their jobs. I submitted a request to take classes that followed these guidelines, but my manager denied it, saying he felt these classes were not necessary. In another department, a manager allowed his employees to take the same classes.

Do I have grounds to take legal action against the company for not following the guidelines and allowing someone else to take the same classes? Or does the company reserve the right to do as it pleases?

—C.B., Los Angeles

A By law an employer must reimburse an employee for all expenses reasonably related to employment.

In your case, however, it sounds like the classes you would like to take are optional. Even though the classes had a "direct relationship" to your job, the issue is whether or not it is a mandatory expense that you are required to incur.

Apparently, your manager did not feel that it was a necessary expense. Just because the employer reimburses employees of other departments for these classes does not mean that you also are eligible. If, however, the reason for this double standard is based in discrimination or whistle-blower retaliation, it would be improper.

> *If you persist in your efforts to seek reimbursement, you might damage your future relations within the company.*

You might be able to claim your employer breached a promise to provide you this type of reimbursement. Your case would be stronger, however, if you had incurred the expense based upon your boss' promises.

Your employer will probably say that the supervisor has the discretion to approve reimbursement for classes on a case-by-case basis. Furthermore, if you persist in your efforts to seek reimbursement, you might damage your future relations within the company. Weigh your desire to take these courses so you can improve your standing with the company against the harm the dispute might cause.

41

SEVERANCE PAY

Severance Pay Isn't a Requirement

Q My daughter had worked four years for an archi-
tectural firm and was recently laid off. She was
given two weeks' pay, which seems rather meager. Is
there anything in the law that defines what severance
should be?

—H.S., Newport Beach

A There is no law governing or even requiring an employer to provide severance pay. However, if an employer has a policy—either in practice or explicitly in an employee handbook—that provides for severance pay, it must be applied equally to all employees.

The severance package offered by the employer may be increased by an employee asserting other claims, such as discrimination, retaliation for whistle-blowing or defamation.

If an employer requires an employee to sign a general release as a condition to receiving severance pay, a full evaluation of all possible rights should be obtained through an attorney. If an employer does not require a general release, an employee can informally try to increase the severance amount and then pursue the employer for more, if justified.

> *If an employer requires an employee to sign a general release as a condition to receiving severance pay, a full evaluation of all possible rights should be obtained through an attorney.*

42
RETIREMENT PLANNING

Retirement Planning? For Some, It's SIMPLE

Q I work for a small TV production company. We do not have a retirement plan. I read recently that the minimum-wage bill included something called SIMPLE (Savings Incentive Match Plan for Employees).

What is that? And how much must my boss contribute?

—S. S., Costa Mesa

A There is no requirement that an employer set up a mandatory retirement plan. However, there are rules that prohibit owners or executives of a company from simply setting up a plan for their own benefit.

If an employer chooses to use a pension or retirement plan, specific rules must be followed. SIMPLE is a retirement plan in which employees can contribute up to $6,000 annually and an employer provides a matching contribution of 2% to 3% of an employee's income.

One advantage of retirement plans is that they allow employees to save money without currently paying taxes on it. Eventually, taxes may have to be paid. But it's better for employees to defer taxes until after retirement, when they presumably would earn less and would fall into a lower tax bracket.

There's also a general rule of thumb that if a person can postpone paying certain taxes for five years and earn interest on those amounts, the amount earned could offset the tax bite.

> *One advantage of retirement plans is that they allow employees to save money without currently paying taxes on it.*

43

PENSION RESTRICTIONS

Employer Can't Limit 401(k) Participation

Q My employer, a Fortune 500 company, will not allow me to participate in the company's 401(k) program because I am below a "manager" level. (I am also represented by a union, but both union and nonunion lower staff employees are prevented from 401(k) participation.)

Since 401(k) plans provide a significant tax shelter for retirement savings, is it legal for the company to exclude certain classes of employees from participating in the 401(k)? Shouldn't all employees be eligible for the same government-regulated tax benefits?

—T.L., Burbank

A Pension plans provide an incentive to accumulate compensation with great tax benefits. Even though the government is giving up immediate taxes, it is easing the burden on its welfare system by encouraging people to plan for their retirement years themselves. It is especially valuable to higher-compensated management personnel of businesses.

As a condition of such favorable tax treatment, however, the government also imposes other rules. Theoretically, the plan cannot discriminate against lower-paid workers. It should include all of its employees.

An employer can temporarily exclude certain employees from participation in the plan by imposing certain qualifications.

It is possible the union may have negotiated different treatment under the plan to gain other benefits or because it has its own plan. Check with your union representative regarding this.

An employer can temporarily exclude certain employees from participation in the plan by imposing certain qualifications such as those regarding age, service with the company or vesting requirements. But if your employer unlawfully discriminates against lower staff employees, the penalties could be very severe, including disqualification of the entire plan for favorable tax treatment.

If your employer unlawfully discriminates against lower staff employees, the penalties could be very severe.

I question whether the plan they have is really a 401(k). If it is a different type of an executive compensation plan or a bonus arrangement, it may be subject to other rules.

Whatever the exact nature of your plan is, the plan document itself should be fully evaluated for its exact specifications. Don't rely upon the oral representations of your management.

44

PENSION PROBLEMS

*Pension Comparison Points Out
a Problem*

Q I retired in 1979 from a large Orange County company after more than 20 years of service. My pension was calculated on a formula that included time of service plus base pay. During the hectic '60s and '70s, employees received numerous cost-of-living raises. In determining my pension, however, the company excluded all cost-of-living raises, maintaining they were not part of my base pay.

A few years after my retirement, I returned as a contract employee. In discussions with my fellow employees who were contemplating retirement I discovered that their pensions were to be considerably more than mine. When I asked, the company said it now incorporates all past cost-of-living increases into the base pay.

I feel that I have been discriminated against, since I received the same cost-of-living increases the later retirees received. Do I have a case here?

—E. C., Laguna Hills

A To really know if you have a case, an attorney would have to thoroughly review and compare your pension plan documents with those of the current employees. I would specifically look for the formula for computing the base pay. You could compare those two documents yourself.

There is a statute of limitation deadline concern. Since you retired around 17 years ago, the company may argue that you have waived any claims related to your rights. Those deadlines would have long since passed.

> *Even if you waived some of your rights for a higher pension benefit for previous years, you still might successfully argue for recent and future years.*

However, you could argue that this is a continuing violation. Even if you might have waived some of your rights for a higher pension benefit for previous years, you still might successfully argue for recent and future years. Also, statute of limitations for fraud commence three years from the date that you have or should have discovered the fraud.

You should also evaluate the damages that you might suffer in the future. If it's a difference of a few hundred dollars a year, then it may not be worth your time or the interest of an attorney to pursue it further. However, if it results in a significant amount of damages to you over the coming years, it may be worth evaluating further. You may want to see an attorney who specializes in Employee Retirement Income Security Act law.

The Labor Code requires payment of all wages upon discharge.

SICKNESS

45

SICK PAY ACCRUAL

Worker Wants Option of Cashing In Days

Q My employer changed our sick leave policy in 1982 after I had accrued six months of sick time, the maximum amount.

The new policy has cash-out provisions, which makes it significantly better. Under the old policy, the accumulated hours were placed in a separate account and could be used only for sick time durations longer than seven days, hospitalizations or for the death of a family member. For all practical purposes, I cannot and have never been able to use any significant amounts of my previously accrued hours.

Can an employer change a policy retroactively for a previously accrued benefit? These hours should be made available or they should allow me to cash them out.

—B.K., Newport Beach

A Even though the question is not totally clear, it sounds like you want to make the employer's new policy apply retroactively to your previous accrued benefits.

It can happen that way if the employer meant it to be. How your previous accrued benefits are handled depends upon the contractual commitments of the employer at that time.

How your previous accrued benefits are handled depends upon the contractual commitments of the employer at that time.

It appears that those accrued benefits were subject to several conditions for which you have never qualified. Not only does it seem to be difficult to refit those old benefits into the new program, but it may create some hard feelings between you and your employer in the process.

Additionally, there may be a problem on timing. If you first asked the employer to apply the new rule to the old benefits more than four years ago and they refused at that time, you may have lost your rights to complain.

Regardless, it sounds like you can still take advantage of those benefits indefinitely in the future if you comply with the requirements. They may continue to be valuable to you in the unfortunate event

Certain accrued benefits such as vacation pay must be paid upon termination of employment.

that you are in a position to ultimately use them. This sounds like insurance—you hate to be in a position to use it, but if you do, you're glad it's there.

Under California law, certain accrued benefits such as vacation pay must be paid upon termination of employment. Other benefits, such as sick pay, may not necessarily be paid on a date of termination, depending upon the employer's contractual policy.

46

SICK PAY

Payment Not Mandated for Accrued
Sick Leave

Q The company I work for allows us six sick days a
year. I have been with this company for more than
16 years. I rarely call in sick, even if I am ill. I now
have accumulated 247 sick hours.

I would like to retire next year, and have been told
that I will lose all of those hours. If I take more than
nine sick days a year, I will be put on corrective action,
in which case I would not be eligible for a raise.

Is this right that I lose these hours and pay for
being a conscientious employee?

—S.S., Moorpark

A To begin with, there is no requirement that an employer provide any paid sick leave. And if paid sick leave is provided, there is no law that you have a right to accrue it from year to year or have it payable upon termination or retirement.

An employer's promises regarding these matters can be enforced, however.

If paid sick leave is provided, there is no law that you have a right to accrue it from year to year.

Apparently, your employer has allowed you to keep accruing sick hours. If the only risk of taking more than nine sick days in a year is that you will not get a raise, you may want to consider taking the sick time after getting your raise. Make sure, however, that taking a great deal of sick leave won't cause your premature termination.

Evaluate whether the leave must actually be for sickness. Some employers actually require a doctor's excuse and a definite medical justification for such leave. Other employers are not so demanding.

Consider using accrued benefits as a bargaining chip for a more favorable retirement and severance package.

Evaluate how other employees have been treated in regard to their sick leave. Has the employer been consistent with you? If there is a double standard, determine why.

Rather than incur the wrath of the employer by taking excessive sick pay, consider using that accrued benefit as a bargaining chip for a more favorable retirement and severance package. If the employer knows that you could theoretically disrupt the work flow at work by taking substantial leave until the date of your retirement, they might appreciate your honesty and reward you.

In the end, it might be better for your employer to speed up your retirement and bring in someone else who will be a consistent and steady worker.

47

HEALTH INSURANCE

Don't Take Boss' Word About Health Coverage

Q Recently, I was notified by my employer, who has less than 20 employees, that I am no longer covered under the group medical health plan. I was involved in a serious accident and was in the process of undergoing intensive treatment to regain the use of my arm. Now, I can't obtain medical treatment necessary for my recovery.

I have been unable to work during this time and will not be able to perform my usual job duties. What are my options to obtain the medical treatment needed for my recovery?

—P.B., Covina

A Loss of medical coverage is a serious matter. Don't take your employer's word that you are no longer covered under the group plan. Review the plan yourself. Call the health carrier to determine their position. Determine why you have been dropped from the plan.

There are many reasons why an employee can be dropped from a plan, including failure to continue employment. Evaluate the promises of your employer. Does your employer have a written policy providing for continued coverage in the event of medical leave? Did the employer ever tell you orally about such a policy?

There are many reasons why an employee can be dropped from a plan.

If your employer treated you improperly in the workplace on other occasions, this may provide additional leverage to negotiate for continued health coverage.

If your disability was caused by a workplace accident, you might qualify for workers' compensation benefits that include payment for medical bills. There are many government programs, such as Medicare or MediCal, that provide for medical treatment, depending upon your age.

If your disability was caused by a workplace accident, you might qualify for workers' compensation benefits that include payment for medical bills.

Employers with more than 20 workers usually must notify employees that they have "COBRA rights," which allow employees to pay for continuation of coverage for up to 18 months. Since your employer has fewer than 20 employees, this probably does not apply.

48

COBRA INSURANCE BENEFITS

Insurance Not Certain for Fired Pregnant Worker

Q My wife is pregnant and works for a bank that is supposed to be sold at the end of October. They're telling her that when the bank is sold, she will have no rights to insurance or COBRA. Is that true?

—V.N., Rossmoor

A COBRA benefits are available to eligible employees to allow them to continue health coverage under an employer's group health plan after termination of employment. There are no COBRA benefits without a group health plan. According to the Office of Pension & Welfare Benefit Administration, if an employer discontinues its group health plan, the employees do not have a right to continue coverage under the COBRA provisions. If the new owners do provide a group health plan, your wife would be eligible for COBRA benefits.

> *There are no COBRA benefits without a group health plan.*

A union contract might prevent an employer from eliminating or changing a group health plan. The new owner may also be obligated to continue the benefits if it simply is buying the stock of the existing bank, as opposed to just the assets.

You may be able to acquire insurance for your wife under the group health plan at your employer. Contact your benefits administrator about adding your wife to the policy. Some plans allow you to add dependents to your coverage, even if it is not time for open enrollment, if there has been a substantial life change.

> *If an employer discontinues its group health plan, employees do not have a right to continue coverage under COBRA.*

The loss of a spouse's job and insurance benefits sometimes qualifies. Also, if your wife finds a new job elsewhere, some insurance plans may provide coverage without a pre-existing condition exclusion.

49

DISABILITY INSURANCE

State Disability Refund if '95 Cap Was Exceeded

Q What is the maximum amount a single employer was allowed to deduct from my wages for State Disability Insurance in 1995? If I have a refund due, from whom can I collect?

—J.W., Newport Beach

A State Disability Insurance (SDI) provides benefits to eligible workers experiencing a loss of wages when they are unable to perform their usual work because of pregnancy, nonoccupational illness or nonoccupational injury.

State Disability Insurance (SDI) provides benefits for pregnancy, nonoccupational illness or nonoccupational injury.

Disability insurance is paid for by employees who contribute through payroll deductions. For some workers, disability insurance costs are a fringe benefit paid for by the employer.

The maximum amount a single employer could deduct from SDI in 1995 was $317.67. If you have a refund due, you can claim it on your state tax return as "excess SDI." You will receive a refund from the Franchise Tax Board.

[In 1998, the maximum income amount which can be deducted is $158.84. This is calculated by taking .5% of the employee's income up to a maximum income of $31,767.]

50
WORKERS' COMP. CLAIMS

Employer Balking at Workers' Comp. Claim

Q My wife, a petroleum saleswoman, sustained injuries while driving her car performing work duties. The other party was insured and the insurance company has admitted complete liability.

My wife's employer has requested she not file a workers' compensation claim and instead encouraged her to pursue State Disability Insurance benefits. If she pursues the SDI benefits, will this prevent her from pursuing a workers' comp. claim?

Is she entitled to unemployment benefits? Her employer has also refused to pay for any sick days even though she has worked for the company for six years and only missed two days.

—D.R., Long Beach

A It is wrong for an employer to insist that a worker file a claim under SDI. Once you select those benefits, it may be difficult, if not impossible, to make a claim later for workers' compensation benefits.

SDI benefits are often easier to obtain than workers' compensation benefits. SDI, however, has a lower weekly benefit. Also, benefits under workers' compensation can continue indefinitely, even for the rest of your life if necessary. SDI benefits are limited to one year.

Since the injury was work related, the claim should be filed through the workers' compensation system. For an employer to encourage you otherwise may constitute fraud on the SDI system, which obtains some of its funds from the state.

You might want to evaluate the reasons why your wife's employer is encouraging her not to file for workers' compensation benefits. If it is because the employer did not follow laws insuring her under such a program, the employer could be subjected to a mandatory fine of $10,000 and other penalties as well.

I suggest that she respond to her employer's request in writing. She should inform her supervisor that since the accident was in fact work related, she is required by law to submit it to the workers' compensation system instead of the state disability system.

Also, I suggest putting the request for sick pay in writing. Evaluate the company's policy for medical leave and sick pay. The company might have a short-term disability program that would provide more money than the other systems. Very often a worker might continue to receive full salary for a period of time, followed by a percentage of his or her salary under a long-term disability program.

If an employer has 50 or more employees and an employee has worked there for more than one year, the employer may be required to return the worker to the same job after the medical leave.

51

WORKERS' COMP. DEADLINES

Timeliness Can Be Critical in Filing Worker Claims

Q I was a quality engineer and was offered and accepted a technician supervisor job because they were going to take me off salary and place me on hourly wages.

Around midnight one night, I was moving a piece of equipment that weighed about 400 or 500 pounds and hurt my neck and back.

My doctor sent letters to my company advising them that I should slow down and stop lifting. The company just kept pushing. I turned in a two-week notice, but the doctor did not tell me he was putting me on disability a week before I was to quit.

This happened in 1990. My understanding was when I finished (trade) school in 1992 I would have a job. At present I am still unemployed.

I am now on general relief to get medical help for my back. At present, I cannot do physical labor. I also believe my age is a problem. I am 57.

I am not sure if I have any rights. Do I?

—K.O., Norwalk

A It appears that many of your rights may have been violated by your former employer. However, the problem is not particularly which rights you have, but the enforcement of them. The law requires that people must take appropriate legal action regarding a violation of rights within a certain period of time. If such deadlines are not met, the right becomes unenforceable. Even though there are many exceptions, the statute of limitation deadlines generally are one year for breach of rights involving a workers' compensation claim or a tort, two years for a breach of an oral contract, three years for fraud or statutory violations and four years for a breach of a written contract.

It appears that most of your claims have long since passed any applicable statute of limitation period. Assuming that you did not have a statute of limitation problem, you might have had many enforceable rights.

Laws governing overtime work require that you should have been given additional compensation either at time and a half or double time, depending upon the number of hours that you were putting in.

You make reference to an injury sustained at work. It is illegal for a company to retaliate against you because of your attempts to file a workers' compensation claim or because of your medical disability.

I am unclear as to whether you have continued on work disability or on a workers' compensation claim since the date you left your employment. If you had appropriately filed a workers' compensation claim, then your claims may continue for an indefinite time as long as you are disabled. Additionally, workers' compensation claimants have various rights to reinstatement once the disability has been resolved.

One of the biggest problems in all employee rights matters is timeliness. Victims of workplace wrongs need to be continually reminded to promptly evaluate their claims and to either waive them or try to resolve them before statutory deadlines pass.

52
WORKERS' COMP. RETALIATION

Workers' Comp. Claim Might Not Save Job

Q I was injured at work in July 1995, and required knee surgery. After the surgery, my doctor told me there was so much damage to my cartilage that I would require a complete knee replacement sometime in the future. My knee is still causing me a lot of pain and it looks as if I will need surgery sooner rather than later.

Can I be laid off while I am recovering from surgery?.

—S.R., Lake Forest

A An employer can't retaliate against an employee for filing a workers' compensation claim for a work injury. A company might be able to claim that you would have been laid off even if you had not been injured, attributing the layoff to an economic business decision.

> An employer can't retaliate against an employee for filing a workers' compensation claim for a work injury.

However, it could be argued that it would be premature for a company to lay you off while you are on leave. It's possible, for example, that your job might reopen by the time you are ready to return to work. Rather than laying off someone who is on such a leave, most smart employers will wait until the return date and evaluate jobs and openings at that time.

Employers with more than 50 employees may be subject to the Family and Medical Leave Act, which requires that the company return a worker to his or her former position within 12 weeks of beginning such a leave. Even though more than 12 weeks may have elapsed for you, the employer may have failed to comply with precise notices that are required before the 12-week period can start.

> Employers may be subject to the Family and Medical Leave Act, which requires the company return a worker to his or her former position.

You should also look at the employee handbook or benefits guide to determine if there is an internal policy regarding work injury or medical leave. It's possible that policies in the handbook may prevent the employer from laying you off.

There is no requirement that an employer provide any paid sick leave.

LEAVES

53

MEDICAL ACCOMMODATION

Sometimes It's Worth Quitting,
Starting Over

Q I have worked for the same company for seven years, and for the last two years I've been traveling for them. For 15 months I was on the road at least 400 days, expected to work at least 6 days a week and 12 hours a day.

After a number of attempts to get out of my position and into a stable working environment, I was told I am not really "company material," but if I keep up the good work maybe in six to nine months I can prove myself.

On the brink of suicide, I was given some vacation time and then placed under a doctor's care. After three months, the doctor has released me back to work as long as I don't travel.

The company wrote me a letter stating that, since I can no longer do the job they hired me for, they are refilling my position on a permanent basis and they have no jobs for me. They are talking about a termination severance package.

Is this right?

—W. M., Palm Springs

A The key to asserting any employee rights is under-standing the hidden reasons behind any unfair acts of the employer. On the surface, it appears your company simply does not have a position open for you after you unilaterally took an extended leave.

Since the company challenged you to "keep up the good work" to prove yourself as "company material," evaluate your work performance. Has it been good enough over an extended period of time to justify you asking for another position in the company? If there is another position open, compare your qualifications with whomever gets the job.

Laws require return to the same job after medical leave up to 12 weeks.

There are state and federal laws that require an employer to return an employee to his or her same job after medical leave up to 12 weeks. In your situation, it is not clear whether your leave, in addition to your vacation time, exceeded 12 weeks.

Even if it did not, your previous job is no longer available, and your employer claims no other jobs are available, either. Ask some of your friends to determine if that is true.

Your employer might have an obligation to "reasonably accommodate" you in another position. If your medical condition was in fact caused by work and qualifies under the worker's compensation laws, your employer has additional responsibilities to put you back to work, even in another position.

Evaluate the termination severance package. Try to negotiate one with higher payments to you. See an attorney.

In retrospect, getting a fair severance, leaving the company, and starting a new life with other employment might be the best thing for you. Despite its potential unfairness, it is certainly better than enduring continued stress.

54
MEDICAL LEAVE REPRISALS

Laws Protect Against
Medical Leave Reprisals

Q I have had difficulty recovering from surgery I had six months ago, which kept me out of work (on medical leave) for five weeks. My doctors have recommended follow-up surgery to help correct the problems.

I am employed by a multibillion-dollar company. My supervisor threatened my job if I go out on medical leave again. I reported him to Human Resources, which said they would talk to him.

I understand that the company cannot fire me if I have this surgery and abide by the company's policy of providing 30-day notice of medical leave, but what else can they do? Am I due any damages for my boss's blatantly illegal conduct? What courses of action would you recommend?

—N. N., Orange County

A It is illegal for your employer to fire or otherwise retaliate against you for taking appropriate medical leave. Laws generally provide a leave period of 12 weeks. Protection while on this leave applies whether the injury or illness was caused as a result of work or for other reasons.

If your leave is caused by a workplace injury, there are other laws as well that give you protection from retaliation.

Simply because your boss threatened to fire you doesn't give you any claim for damages. Your damages have not yet occurred. It certainly is an indication of his attitude, however.

Make sure you understand the company's policy on medical leave and comply with all of its specific requirements. Keep past employment reviews at home.

Accordingly, you should document his statement to you in a letter to him directly or to the Human Resources Department. Don't simply rely on an oral complaint to the Human Resources Department. Make sure you understand the company's policy on medical leave and comply with all of its specific requirements. Ask the Human Resources Department for the rules and the federal or state leave laws as well.

Keep past employment reviews at home. Maintain a diary so that you can document any change in the manner you are treated by your boss.

It's a good possibility that your boss simply did not know the law involved or your company rules on such leaves. If he's informed that he simply can't retaliate against you for a leave protected by law, then hopefully there will be little problem in the future.

FAMILY LEAVE

Family Leave Rights Not Employer's Option

Q I have two children under three years old and my wife is going to have another baby. I asked my supervisor to give me a two-week leave to take care of my wife and two little children. But my supervisor would give me only one day and said he will document me as "absent without excuse" if I take more than that.

Do I have the right to ask for maternity leave or family leave?

—M.T., Victorville

A You may have substantial leave rights pursuant to federal and state law. Both the Congress and the state Legislature have enacted laws entitling an employee with at least a year's tenure to 12 weeks of leave for certain designated purposes at businesses with 50 or more employees. There are other require-ments as well. An employee can take up to 12 weeks of leave during any 12-month period. Both laws allow leave for care of a newborn child or of a spouse with a "serious health condition." Leave is even allowed for an employee's own serious health condition.

Both the Congress and the state Legislature have enacted laws entitling an employee with at least a year's tenure to 12 weeks of leave for certain designat-ed purposes at businesses with 50 or more employees.

Upon returning from such a leave, you would generally be enti-tled to the same or equivalent posi-tion. Retaliation against you for taking leave is prohibited.

The two-week leave that you requested appears to be well within the 12-week requirement. However, you do not state how incapacitated your wife really is. If she is going to have a baby eight months from now, it may be harder to justify leave on these grounds than if she is bedridden or about to give birth. You have to establish that she has a serious health condition that makes your presence necessary.

Aside from the laws, evaluate the policy of your own company. Look at the employee handbook to see what type of personal leave is allowed.

If your supervisor documents you as "absent with-out an excuse," ask for elaboration. Does this mean that they intend to fire you because of it? Will this affect your next review?

You might want to send him or her a polite letter about the laws that I have just described, and ask the company to reconsider its policy.

6

MEDICAL LEAVE

Right to Extended Leave for Health Prescribed by Law

Q My wife just returned to work after being off on medical leave. Prior to that, she took sick leave ranging from one day to three consecutive days. Upon her return, she was warned that if she took leave again, she would be terminated according to the company policy. Is this legal?

—M., Lake Forest

A It is illegal for an employer to discriminate or retaliate against an employee who has taken medical
leave for a duration allowed by state or federal law.

Even though there are some
exceptions based upon extreme
hardship to the employer, employees have many rights to a leave
period of twelve weeks or more,
depending on the type of illness
and applicability of state or federal
law.

> *It is the
> employer's
> responsibility to
> apply the leave
> to state or
> federal law.*

In your wife's situation, if she
has not used up her authorized
leave according to state or federal law, it would be
improper for the company to terminate her for additional sick leave.

Keep in mind that it is the employer's responsibility to apply the leave to state or federal law.

If the company fails to document it in writing, her rights to the
full leave period may continue to be
preserved from day to day.

If she has already used up all
the leave that she is authorized to
use according to law, the employer
may be entitled to terminate her for
excessive absenteeism.

Since her employer threatened
termination if sick leave happened
again, much of your wife's rights
depend on her rights to legal leave
on the date that it occurs in the
future.

> *If she has
> already used up
> all the leave that
> is authorized
> according to law,
> the employer may
> be entitled to ter-
> minate her for
> excessive absen-
> teeism.*

Also determine whether the company is applying a
double standard and treating your wife more harshly
than other employees.

57
MEDICAL LEAVE MISTAKES

*Medical Leave Mistakes Easy
for Firm to Make*

Q While I was out on medical disability for severe depression, I received a letter from the company saying that I must return to work July 12. My doctor faxed back that I would not return until August 30.

I was fired. When I applied for unemployment, however, I was told that I had failed to return to work. Can a company fire you while you are on a medical leave?

—J. L., Monrovia

A There are many ways in which your company may have acted improperly in firing you while you were on medical leave. Review disability and other contractual policies to determine whether you are protected from being terminated while on medical leave.

If your medical condition results from your work

environment, your leave might more appropriately fall under workers' compensation rules. The law restricts an employer from retaliating against an employee who pursues workers' compensation rights. There are limits, however, depending upon the length of the leave and the reasonable needs of the company.

The Americans with Disabilities Act ("ADA") requires employers to "reasonably accommodate" certain workers with specified disabilities. ADA issues usually arise when there are physical limitations on an employee's work abilities. It will be argued, however, that severe depression may not be covered under that law.

The Americans with Disabilities Act (ADA) requires employers to "reasonably accommodate" certain workers with specified disabilities.

According to the Federal Family and Medical Leave Act and its California counterpart, employees in companies with at least 50 employees can take up to 12 weeks' leave for disability reasons. The employee needs to work a certain number of hours in a year and the illness needs to be of a certain severity to qualify. If the facts of your case apply, the company is required to return you to your former position if you are able to return within 12 weeks of your disability.

It is very easy for a business to make a mistake in applying these laws. For example, it is the employer's responsibility to notify you that your leave qualifies under this law and is being counted against the 12-week allocation. The 12-week leave doesn't begin until the company provides this written notice. If the company fires you before the 12-week period expires, it could be liable for wrongful termination.

With a variety of laws protecting you, there is a good chance that your company can't fire you while you're on medical leave.

The key to asserting any employee rights is understanding the hidden reasons behind any unfair acts of the employer.

DISCRIMINATION

58

SEXUAL HARASSMENT

Workstation Pinups May Be
Sexual Harassment

Q I work part time and don't have a desk of my own. When I'm in the office, I sit at a colleague's desk and use his computer.

I'm uncomfortable because he has taped up several magazine cutouts of women in various poses and states of undress.

I had been taking the pictures down while I'm working, then taping them back up when I leave.

But my colleague has started complaining about that and making snide remarks about me. What can I do?

—C.B., Newport Beach

A There is hardly any doubt that such pinups are in fact sexual harassment. In 1993, the U.S. Supreme Court ruled that sexual harassment can be "environmental" and does not require a direct, unwanted sexual advance. All that is required is that a reasonable person would consider the workplace hostile. Graphic pinups, continuously displayed, are both offensive and humiliating to most women. The offender's snide remarks obviously interfere with work performance.

All that is required is that a reasonable person would consider the workplace hostile.

I would suggest that you put your complaint in writing, not only regarding the offensive pictures but regarding the comments that were made as well. This way there will be no doubt that the company itself has been placed on notice of the offensive conduct.

This is also important in giving the employee additional rights if there is any retaliation at all because of the complaint. If the company does not act appropriately, the employee should consider filing a complaint with the Department of Fair Employment and Housing or consult an attorney.

59

HARASSMENT OPTIONS

Suspect Harassment? Proceed With Caution

Q I have been a support-staff employee at the same law firm for the better part of 20 years and, given my maximum pension-vesting and vacation days, have reason to suspect that management has been instructed to induce me to resign or to terminate my employment.

In recent months, I have been assigned several projects at a time, all with similar deadlines. I can meet most—but not all—of the deadlines. I am invariably reprimanded for failing to meet all deadlines, yet management will not authorize overtime for me or hire temporary help.

Inasmuch as I am over 40, I am highly unlikely to be hired by other law firms. I have written to the California Labor Commissioner, only to be told that its personnel can be of no assistance. Can any other government agency be of assistance? Should I hire a lawyer?

—J.S., Mar Vista

A Unfortunately, employers sometimes resort to harassment to try to force employees to quit. Although the California Labor Commissioner apparently was unable to assist you, it should not be implied that the office was avoiding you. The Labor Commissioner is not set up to assist on discrimination claims unless they are based on the whistleblowing or a similar type of activity by the employee. If the harassment arises out of discrimination, the appropriate state agency is the Department of Fair Employment and Housing.

A lawyer can help you understand your rights in the workplace while you are still employed. In fact, lawyers like to get involved in a case before a termination or resignation occurs. Much more evidence of the employer's wrongdoing can be obtained if the employee is still working there than if employment has ended.

The real challenge is what to do about the problem while you are still there. You indicate that you would like to retain the job but solve the problem. You need to be very diplomatic.

Present your claims and concerns in writing to your supervisor. If the firm gives you too many assignments and you can't meet all of your deadlines, ask for a clarification of priorities. Document any differences between the way the firm treats you and others. Try to determine the reason you are being harassed. That might make a big difference in how you respond.

If you are being harassed by one particular supervisor, consider approaching that person privately about the problem. You might "win more points" that way than you would by going over his or her head. However, if you need to, go up the ladder of authority to discuss your problem.

Review the employee handbook for employer rules regarding this type of treatment. If there is an internal grievance procedure, consider using it.

An attorney's letter to management can accomplish a lot, but can also ruin your future with the employer. Employers seldom forget an employee who has threatened a lawsuit or who appears to have a lawyer ready to make a claim at the slightest mistake.

60

PREGNANCY DISCRIMINATION

*Pregnancy Leave No Ground
for Discrimination*

Q I am more than four months' pregnant. My doctor has put me on bed rest because of extremely high blood pressure, passing out, dizziness and vomiting. Can my employer terminate me due to "hardship to the company" or, when I return to work, reduce my pay and job responsibilities, even if I have a full release from my doctor to go back to work with no restriction?

I am an accounting clerk. The company has about 50 employees, but it is moving out of state in May.

— E.M., Huntington Beach

According to Federal Law, employers cannot discriminate against pregnant employees if the employer has 15 or more workers. According to state law, if the employer has at least five employees the employer cannot so discriminate and must give you up to four months of leave for a pregnancy-related illness. Such leave does not need to be taken at one time.

According to state law, if the employer has at least five employees, the employer must give you up to four months of leave for a pregnancy-related illness.

Other federal and state legislation has provided another twelve weeks worth of leave to care for yourself or your family. In total, a pregnant person might claim seven months of leave.

Upon your return to your work, the employer must return you to your former job unless your job has been eliminated for reasons other than your leave or there is a reasonable hardship for the employer to hold your job open rather than leaving it either unfilled or filling it with temporary employees.

The employer's finances and size may be a factor in deciding what is in fact a reasonable hardship. If the employer cannot return you to your former job, you must be returned to a substantially similar job unless one is not available or if one is available, giving such a job to you would again be a reasonable hardship. Often it is very difficult for the employer to justify not giving you such a job.

The employer must return you to your former job unless your job has been eliminated or there is a reasonable hardship for the employer to hold your job open.

If the company is moving out of the state, the employer has to give you the same opportunities to move with the company that it gives its other employees who are not pregnant.

61

BIAS AND AT-WILL STATUS

"At-Will" Workers Still Can Prove Bias if Fired

Q It is my understanding that if you are an "at-will" employee, your employer can terminate you at any time without warning and without reason. If that is the case, then it seems that it would be perfectly legal for an employer to terminate an employee based on race, religion, national origin, age or gender as long as the employer does not explicitly say so, or does not practice this type of termination enough times to establish a statistical pattern that may be detected by an Equal Employment Opportunity Commission investigation.

I would like to know what you think, because the "at-will" clause allows employers, in my opinion, to drive a truck through the Equal Employment Opportunity laws that are supposed to protect employees.

—S.A., Costa Mesa

A There is no doubt that in California there is a basic presumption that everyone who can be terminated with or without cause is an "at-will" employee. And employers can avoid Equal Employment Opportunity sanctions unless there is proof of discrimination, illegal retaliation, or a violation of contractual promises to terminate employees only for good cause.

Make note of jokes, stories, comments and profanity that show bias.

It's easier to provide proof than you might think, however. "Circumstantial evidence" can be a convincing, useful tool. Perry Mason seldom had a murderer admit guilt at the beginning of the television show. It was only after piecing together alibis, footprints, fingerprints, eyewitness testimony and other evidence that he was able to prove his case.

In proving discrimination, it certainly helps to have statistical evidence of a pattern of discrimination. You might make note of jokes, stories, comments and profanity

Make a chart and compare yourself with your peers.

that show bias. Interview others at work to determine if they perceive a biased attitude the same as you do.

Make a chart and compare yourself with your peers. Was there a double standard? Did they treat you differently than other people? How do you compare in terms of education, tenure with the company, tenure on your particular job, benefits, ways in which you are treated, and most importantly, performance? The more obvious the difference between you and your peers, the easier it might be for you to prove discrimination.

Equal Employment Opportunity laws are alive and well in California. Employment discrimination cases are won every week. Employees have more rights today than ever. The challenge is to fully understand and apply them.

62
RELIGIOUS/ POLITICAL BIAS

Company Can Enforce Its Charitable Impulse

Q I work as a checker in a large grocery chain. During one of the summer months, our employer wants us to urge our customers to contribute to a charitable organization. This bugs me and I think would make my customers uncomfortable. Do employers have the right to expect this from us?

— S.M., Huntington Beach

A According to statute, it is illegal for an employer to retaliate against an employee on the basis of religion or politics. If the reason that you are bothered by the request of your employer is because your own religious or political background conflicts with a particular charity chosen by the employer, then you have every reason to object.

It is illegal for an employer to retaliate against an employee on the basis of religion or politics.

If you don't like the idea simply because you feel that you would be bothering the customers and for no other reason, then the employer can impose this requirement on you.

As a practical answer, evaluate the potential harm to your future with the company if you complain about its requests. Perhaps there is a way that you can make your employer happy by soliciting the customers but doing so in a low-key way that would not annoy them.

63
AIDS BIAS

Confront Bias Toward HIV-Positive Employee

Q One of my co-workers is HIV positive and he encounters a lot of discrimination from the other workers in the company. What should be done to deal with this?

—H.B., Riverside

A California and federal law prohibits discrimination in the workplace. AIDS or HIV-positive status is a protected disability under these laws.

Since the first goal should be to stop the harassment and continue on the job, the victim should consider confronting those doing the harassing. Sometimes a private, person-to-person request accomplishes a lot more than threats or going over someone's head. The victim could share his or her inner hurt feelings about the harassment. I realize this has nothing to do with law, but it might be the best approach to solve the problem. If that doesn't work, make a more formal request in writing to the offending worker.

> *Sometimes a private, person-to-person request accomplishes a lot more than threats or going over someone's head.*

Another option is to talk to management (documented by a follow-up letter) or send a written complaint to the company. If a supervisor is harassing the worker, the company is liable, whether or not it knows about the incidents. If the worker is being harassed by a peer, company officials are liable only if they learn about the wrongful treatment and then fail to reasonably do something about it.

Document the wrongful actions taken. Keep a diary of the history of the problem. Obtain addresses of relevant witnesses and enlist their cooperation. Review company policy regarding discrimination.

A claim can be filed with the Department of Fair Employment and Housing within a year of the discriminatory act. If there is discrimination because of sexual orientation, a claim can be made to the Labor Commissioner's office within 30 days of the discriminatory act. A civil lawsuit also could be filed within one year.

64

AGE

QUESTION

Government, Special Jobs May Require
Applicant's Age

Q I have recently filled out an application for Federal Employment (SF 171), and one of the first items asked for was my date of birth. Is it legal to require this information on an application form?

—A.H., Irvine

A It is normally improper to ask a person's age on an employment application as it is considered good evidence of age discrimination.

However, there are exceptions to that rule. Occasionally, such questions, especially with the federal government, might be reasonably required because of the work involved. The availability of insurance for that particular job might depend on the applicant's age. Certain types of jobs, in fact, might have restrictions because of the special physical conditions of the job. Some employers are required to ask a question that seems discriminatory on its face to comply with affirmative action requirements.

Even though there are many rules in this and other areas that apply to employers as a whole, very often the federal government carves out an exception for itself. On the other hand, as a general rule, government employers are subject to even more stringent rules than required in the private sector.

It is normally improper to ask a person's age on an employment application though there are exceptions to that rule. Occasionally, such questions might be reasonably required because of the work involved.

65

PROVING DISCRIMINATION

*Age Discrimination Illegal,
but Hard to Prove*

Q I was employed by a company for 17 years in an executive management position, then demoted to a sales representative with a contract for an assigned territory.

During the next nine months, the territory was reduced and there was not enough left to make a living. I was forced to look elsewhere for employment. No changes were made to the contract.

This was also done to others in my age group, the late 50s and 60s. In some cases, we were replaced by much younger personnel.

The company made comments to others that we no longer fit their image, even though we performed well and their new personnel have not been able to match our sales figures at all.

I have not been able to obtain a job that pays anywhere near what I had been earning, and have lost all benefits including medical, pension, etc. Is this type of action allowed?

—D.M., Cypress

A It is illegal for an employer to discriminate against an employee based on age. The problem is proving it. The age discrimination laws in California apply only to those who are over the age of 40. There is no maximum limit.

It sounds like you have some good evidence of age discrimination. Age-related statements that you "no longer fit their image" show their bias. Your good past performance and the poor performance of your replacements also are relevant, as well as the statistical information showing that the company is terminating older workers.

It is illegal for an employer to discriminate against an employee based on age. The problem is proving it.

You should either file an age claim with the state Department of Fair Employment and Housing or the federal Equal Employment Opportunity Commission, or seek the advice of an attorney. If you fail to act within one year of your termination, the deadline for claiming your rights will pass.

66

BIASED
PROMOTIONS

*Unclear If Promotions Reflect
Age Bias*

Q I have been employed by a major corporation for over 30 years, the last 27 years in a management position in one department. I have received glowing annual performance ratings from various supervisors who have headed the department.

Recently I found out that very quietly, without any announcement, about 50% of my peers in the department have been upgraded to the next highest management level. I am 57 years old. Everyone upgraded is younger and very few, if any, could match my continuously high performance rating, my varied skills and experience level.

This obvious choice of youth and disregard of over three decades of outstanding service clearly indicates an orchestrated effort by the current managers to force the "old-timer" into an early retirement.

Are we talking age discrimination here? Are any labor laws broken? Do I have any legal recourse?

—G.J., Alta Loma

A It is illegal to discriminate against any employee on the basis of age. The challenge is to show that age was the reason that the others were promoted. You should evaluate all other possible factors for the promotion of those other employees. Compare your salaries, job responsibilities, and performance.

The challenge is to show that age was the reason others were promoted. Evaluate all other possible factors for the promotion of other employees.

Your case would be stronger if peers who were not promoted are in your age category. It hurts your case if some are younger.

If it was an orchestrated effort to force you into retirement, however, it's difficult to understand why such a move would have been made quietly, as you said. It would have made more sense for them to show favoritism outwardly, or to criticize you in your annual reviews.

Regardless, if you can prove discrimination, you have legal recourse through the Department of Fair Employment and Housing, Equal Employment Opportunity Commission, the company's internal grievance procedure, or an attorney.

67

OVER-
QUALIFICATION
BIAS

*Proving Bias Is Hard But
Not Impossible*

Q How do you prove age discrimination? If you're applying for jobs and you sense you're being screened out for being overqualified, is that legal? After a career in the private sector, I want to work in the public sector, but I'm afraid all people see is my age on the application. Is there a recourse?

—B.W., Laguna Beach

❖ ❖ ❖

Proving age discrimination is often very difficult, especially when hiring is involved. Discrimination against present employees is easier to prove because you often have a history of a "double standard," as well as willing witnesses to support your claim.

One way to document where you stand, in a hiring situation, is to compare yourself with the other applicants for the position by striking up a conversation with them in the waiting room before or after your interview. Also, ask anyone you know who actually works for the employer to give you feedback about the identity and qualifications of the person who ultimately gets the job.

If you think that the prospective employer is not considering you because of your age, you could file a complaint with the California Department of Fair Employment and Housing or the federal Equal Employment Opportunity Commission. They have the ability to require the employer to provide all relevant information regarding the job. As an alternative, you can get further information by filing a lawsuit.

You can try to prevent discrimination by not emphasizing age factors. Instead of putting down the dates of previous employment, you might consider being more general. If the employment application asks questions about your age or requires your photograph, from which age can be determined, the employer may be in violation of law. On the other hand, some employers, especially in government, might be required to ask you questions regarding your age, or for that matter race, to comply with affirmative action programs.

Keep in mind that in regard to hiring or promotions, it may not make any difference if the person selected for the job is, in fact, better qualified than you. The law protects your chance to try out for a position. If you have been denied that opportunity for discriminatory reasons, then you may recover damages.

68

MAKING BIAS CLAIMS

Evaluate Facts Before Claiming Bias

Q I am a 51-year-old professional design engineer who has taught at a California community college since 1989. I have been informed that the sections of my classes do not have sufficient enrollment and will be canceled.

This is the policy of the college and the condition of my employment. However, the lead instructor has told me that the remaining students will be transferred to another instructor who was hired recently. He has never taught at the college level.

A labor attorney I spoke to said he didn't think he could pursue a discrimination charge without more information. A person at the state Fair Employment and Housing Department said someone would call me regarding my concerns about age discrimination.

Do I have to investigate to find out this other instructor's age? If so, how would I do it without risking an invasion of privacy charge? Whose obligation is it to prove age discrimination?

—G.P., Irvine

A "Burden of proof" is a legal term that establishes which side has the obligation to prove certain facts. If you desire to pursue an age discrimination claim against your employer, then you need to prove it. Ultimately, it is not sufficient that you simply show that you are over the minimum 40 years of age and that your employer has given preferential treatment to another younger employee. You must also prove that there is no legitimate reason for such a double standard, such as performance, education and other skills that you may not have.

Do an adequate investigation before filing a lawsuit.

You can learn much about another person without invading their privacy. Why not simply talk to some of your friends at the college and try to find out the age and skills of the other instructor? Look for other factors of his selection over you. Is he a friend of your supervisor? Has there been any hint of other bias towards you in the past? Your description of the facts does not tell us whether you are a man or a woman. Are they preferring to replace you because the other instructor is a man and you are a woman?

In evaluating your case, you need to consider other factors. Claims against public entities, such as a community college, may have special requirements. You may be required, for example, to file a notice of your claim within a short time period. It is not unusual for instructors at colleges to have a year-to-year written contract. If this applies to you, you need to closely evaluate your rights as specified in that contract.

It is to your benefit to do an adequate investigation before filing a lawsuit against them. If you ultimately lose, your opponent could sue you for their attorney's fees as well as damages from malicious prosecution and other claims.

Employees have more rights today than ever. The challenge is to fully understand and apply them.

WHISTLE-BLOWING

69

WHISTLE-BLOWER RIGHTS

Fired Whistle-blower May Find Help in Law

Q As controller for a nonprofit company, I became aware of some suspicious bonuses issued to three top executives, including my boss, about four years ago. I asked the outside auditors if the board had approved these bonuses. I later learned that the auditors had spoken to the chief executive officer about the unapproved bonuses but never contacted the board of directors.

About two years later, on the day that my boss retired, the CEO told me to start looking for a new job. Six months later, I was fired and received a severance package.

Later, I told one of the board members about the bonuses. He said another board member had approved over $1 million in executive bonuses, including $500,000 to the CEO, without informing the other board members. The board member promised to repay all of the bonuses via his will. Can a nonprofit company discharge an employee for informing the board of directors about a significant weakness in internal control? It seems like I was done a grave injustice.

—R.D., Orange

❖   ❖   ❖

A Whistle-blowers do indeed have substantial rights, but the whistle-blowing cannot simply be for any complaint or grievance. It must be based on a violation of statutory or constitutional law.

It is very possible that these bonuses violate the Internal Revenue Code. Perhaps the non-profit company raises money based upon its status, but the reality is that most of its income is paid to its wealthy executives. This may not only result in violation of statutory regulations, but might also be a crime.

> *Whistle-blowers have substantial rights, but the whistle-blowing must be based on a violation of statutory or constitutional law.*

You apparently complained to the board of directors about the problem. According to case law, complaining about illegal activity to current management, even without going to an outside governmental authority, is sufficient for these whistle-blower rights to apply.

As with any case, it is your burden to establish a good link between your initial complaints and the ultimate termination. If there is too long of a period between those two events, you might have trouble convincing a judge or a jury that it is related. Also, your severance package may have included a release of all claims against the company. Evaluate it to see if it includes such language.

You also may have a statute of limitations problem. It appears that you were fired 1½ years ago. Most whistle-blower cases have a one-year deadline for filing a lawsuit.

70

WHISTLE-BLOWER OPTIONS

Possible Whistle-blower Faces Several Options

Q My employer told me that I was being let go for reporting the company and its practices to a federal agency. The company said it had a tape and witnesses. I did make a phone call to the federal agency, but placed the call on my cellular phone.

I am fairly certain that my office telephone was tapped without my knowledge and that is how the company found out, since no one else knew. I believe my employer listened in on a conversation I was having with my husband.

What would you advise me to do?

—N.N., Costa Mesa

A You have many rights against your employer. It is illegal for an employer to retaliate against an employee who complains about an illegality or violation of a "fundamental public policy" based in law or the Constitution. You would not have a claim, though, if the matter you complained about did not turn out to be as serious as you thought it might have been.

Additionally, your employer may have invaded your privacy. It is illegal for your employer to tap your telephone conversations without your consent. If the employer did not actually listen into both conversations but rather taped only your end of the conversation and only in your office, then the issue is whether you had a reasonable expectation of privacy. If you had the conversation with your door open where anyone reasonably could overhear, then the taping of your conversation may not be improper. If someone merely eavesdropped on your end without a tape recording, it would not violate any privacy laws.

You also may have a claim for "constructive defamation" if the employer fired you for alleged improper activity, such as being unable to keep confidences. You should not have been fired for that reason in the first place, but if the former employer casts you in a false light in speaking with prospective employers, you might have a claim for defamation.

As a practical matter, you need to weigh your fiduciary obligations as a chief financial officer and a certified public accountant to maintain confidentiality of your employer against your duty as a citizen to report perceived illegalities. If what you thought was improper was not really illegal or if you did not have a reasonable good faith belief of its illegality, then your employer might report you to the state authority that gave you your license in the first place.

You have a right to look at your employee file. I suggest that you request access to your file in writing. If the employer refuses, you might have a claim for damages or for an order to give you access.

Additionally, consider your damages. If you got a better job the day after you were fired, then a judge or jury might not have much compassion in awarding you money. If, however, it took you an extended period of time to find a replacement job and it is not as good as your prior one, then your damages might be big enough to justify legal action.

If you wanted to pursue the whole scope of your rights, you probably would have to go to a lawyer.

71

WHISTLE-BLOWER DILEMMA

Whistle-blower Wonders What to Tell Future Boss

Q After being wrongfully terminated for "whistle-blowing" from a job where I had worked less than six months, I successfully negotiated a cash settlement of all claims against my former employer, with the help of an attorney. My former boss was also subsequently fired.

What is the best way to handle questions from prospective employers regarding my reasons for leaving an excellent, career-building position after such a short time?

I am concerned that if I explain the full details of my departure, I will be branded a troublemaker. On the other hand, if I simply say that my previous boss and I had "chemistry problems," it seems to raise more questions than it answers. Simply leaving this job off my resume, as some people have suggested, would create a big gap in employment. What do you suggest?

A What to tell prospective employers about past employment is a common dilemma. It may drastically affect your ability to secure other employment.

If you negotiated a settlement with your former employer, there is a good chance it included a confidentiality clause. Both you and the employer may already have an agreement as to how the termination of your employment shall be expressed to prospective employers.

The time to negotiate the very best wording is before you sign a settlement agreement. Often, employers will readily agree to term a firing as a layoff or "reorganization." In the alternative, they may agree to not say anything at all about your departure and give a strictly "neutral" reference. This would leave it up to you to classify your termination as you desire.

Even if you did not enter into an agreement with the employer before, you can still do it now.

It is better not to mention to a future employer that you reached a settlement with your former employer. This might imply that you are an employer attacker and scare them off. The "reorganization" explanation often works well. There is no requirement that you go into great detail as to why you left. It may be better to be as vague as possible.

It also is important to be consistent. It does not reflect well on you if your version about your departure is different from that of the employer. Your former employer should want to help you get other employment to take you off the state unemployment rolls, which affects the previous employer's rates. Likewise, that employer does not want to be sued for defaming you to prospective employers, which is so serious that it carries with it triple damages and a possible criminal charge.

To determine what your former employer is saying about you, consider having a friend call about your application for employment. There are private investigative services that do this for a very low fee.

There is another alternative. If the thing that you complained about was so outrageous, the best policy may be to be totally candid about your whistle-blowing. The employer may appreciate your honesty and attitude.

72

WHISTLE-BLOWER RETALIATION

*Retaliation for Complaints of
Workplace Discrimination*

Q Can an employer discipline or fire me if I have complained about discrimination against another employee?

—P.C., San Juan Capistrano

❖   ❖   ❖

A An employer cannot retaliate against an employee who has complained about workplace discrimination—whether the discrimination concerns that employee or even another employee. There can be no retaliation, such as a demotion, loss of benefits or being terminated.

The complaints need not be made to a government agency or outside the management of the employer. It is sufficient that a complaint is made to a supervisor. Thus, many employees not only have a claim for actual discrimination, but also a claim regarding retaliation because of the complaint, even if the discrimination cannot ultimately be proven. A condition to this is that the discrimination complaint must arise from a "reasonable belief."

The complaints need not be made to a government agency. It is sufficient that the complaint be made to a supervisor.

The problem is proving that the employee has reasonable belief of discrimination, that a complaint actually was made to management, and that retaliation occurred because of the complaint. Documenting such complaints in writing is recommended. Witnesses might be able to substantiate retaliation against an employee.

The California Department of Fair Employment and Housing can help. Through the agency, or with the help of an attorney, benefits or a job can be restored and past wages recovered.

73

WHISTLE-BLOWER DEADLINES

*I Blew the Whistle and Got Demoted.
What Can I Do?*

Q I was employed at a major drug chain as the pharmacist in charge. It soon became evident to me that controlled substances were being refilled with no regard to regulations.

After bringing this to the attention of the pharmacy district supervisor and refusing to continue the practice, I was berated, disciplined and demoted to relief vacation pharmacist. I was also reprimanded for refusing a customer's demand for a two-day supply of medication when no refill existed.

I resigned rather than submit to harassment and abuse. I submitted the violations to the state pharmacy board, which substantiated my charges and found that the pharmacy violated regulations.

But I also would like to see the behavior and wrongdoing of the supervisor made part of his personnel file. This incident occurred four years ago, but the management has swept it under the rug, refusing to recognize the supervisor's dereliction of duty.

—E.B., Anaheim

A It is illegal for an employer to retaliate against an employee who in good faith complains about illegalities in the workplace, if those improprieties are of sufficient public concern and qualify under whistleblower laws.

In this case it appears that the violations of your pharmacy did concern matters of sufficient importance to give you great protection. You could have filed a claim against your former employer because of the harassment and abuse that you tolerated. Your resignation could have been termed as a "constructive wrongful termination."

The problem is that you have passed most legal deadlines for filing a claim. Some cases place a deadline of one year for a whistle-blower retaliation claim. Others set it at three years. You could have a claim for breach of oral contract if made within two years or written contract if made within four years.

Even though you said the wrongdoing occurred four years ago, which would theoretically place you beyond most deadlines, you might fall within the filing period if the retaliation continued beyond the date of the first incident. If your employment contract was with an employer from another state, the deadline may be longer than four years, depending upon the state law.

Regarding your question about making your supervisor's behavior a part of his personnel file, you could write a letter to the company asking it to make a note in his file. If your former employer simply does not want to recognize the supervisor's wrongdoing, however, there is little you can do.

You had your chance when you potentially had power to sue the employer. This could have been negotiated through that process. Certainly, if you had filed a lawsuit, a public record of the supervisor's wrongdoing would have been documented forever.

74

RETALIATION FOR FOLLOWING LAW

Production Problems May Be Owner's Doing

Q The owner of the manufacturing firm for which I work often takes some of the product from a customer's order and sells it to individuals for cash as they walk in, even though he does not run a retail store. He later gets upset with us because the orders are not completed on time. This doesn't seem fair or right. I don't know how to approach him, though. What should I do?

—R.D., Fullerton

A It is illegal to retaliate against an employee for refusing to participate in violations of law in the workplace. It also is improper for the owner to retaliate against you if you complain about reasonably perceived illegalities, even if they are ultimately proven not to be illegal.

It is improper for the owner to retaliate against you if you complain about reasonably perceived illegalities.

It is not clear from the question if the owner is involved in illegalities. Selling items for cash when the owner does not run a retail store appears to imply violation of city or county licensing rules as well as IRS or State Franchise Tax Board fraud. It also may involve fraud on your customers if their orders are being intentionally reduced.

You should not be blamed for the consequences of these possible improprieties. It is important to document your position, however. You might want to write the owner a short note, after keeping a copy,

It is important to document your position.

explaining your concerns about the procedure and production demands. It might include a simple suggestion that the owner increase his stock so that the orders are completed on time.

75

SHAREHOLDER WHISTLE-BLOWING

Minority Shareholder Wants to Blow Whistle

Q I am a shareholder and employee of a small publicly traded company. Essentially, the chief executive officer of the company is running the company for his personal benefit. He tries to boost the stock price temporarily with misleading financial information. He is also paying himself an excessive salary and running his personal expenses through the company.

As a minority shareholder, how do I protect myself, besides selling the shares? Does the Securities and Exchange Commission set out guidelines for the conduct of a CEO? How does the "whistle-blowing" protection work for an employee?

—P.C., Irvine

A You face a common whistle-blower's dilemma. If you try to prevent improprieties or illegalities in the workplace, you may suffer adverse consequences.

It certainly appears the CEO of your company is

violating the law. Intentionally misleading others with financial information may be a violation of criminal and civil securities laws, as well as fraud against shareholders.

If actual illegalities are occurring, or if you reasonably believe they are occurring, the executive or the company cannot retaliate against you for blowing the whistle. You will have legal recourse against them for all of your damages plus other penalties if they do.

You owe a duty to all of the shareholders to provide them with accurate information. You can either resign or adequately inform the other shareholders or directors of his improper actions. Indeed, you may have personal liability for the executive's acts if you are an officer of the company. If you are not an officer of the corporation, you can make a claim as a minority shareholder on behalf of all of the shareholders.

Even though whistle-blowing protection laws can be effective, keep in mind that the "atmosphere" at the company will never be the same.

I would suggest that you initially advise the executive of the improprieties in writing. Keep a copy of your letter at home. Keep a journal of any harassment or retaliation that happens after that date. Consider gathering evidence that documents the illegalities.

Even though whistle-blowing protection laws can be effective, keep in mind that the "atmosphere" at the company will never be the same. The executive may not take the ultimate step of firing you, but he will probably resort to more subtle acts of harassment over a longer period of time to encourage you to quit.

If you ever lose your job, monitor what your former boss is saying about you to prospective employers. There are criminal penalties and triple damages that can be imposed for blacklisting you.

76

WORK INJURY RETALIATION

Job Status of Injured Worker

Q I worked for nearly five years as a truck driver and I injured my back while on the job. I filed a workers' compensation case in 1992. My company sent me the paperwork to terminate my pension/profit-sharing plan, dated back to the date of injury, which I signed for my check to be sent this year.

Would this action be considered grounds for illegal job termination, or was that just the termination of my benefits to the pension/profit-sharing plan?

—G.B., Buena Park

A Simply terminating pension plan benefits does not necessarily mean that you have been terminated from your job. Often, employers may terminate the plan for all of its employees or may have extended to you the option to terminate it prior to the termination of your job, resignation or retirement.

It seems very strange that they would terminate it, however, as of the date of your injury. There are laws that prohibit retaliation against an employee because of a workplace injury. Such retaliation could be your demotion or the loss of some benefits. The deadline for filing a claim for such improper action is one year from the date it was done.

Simply terminating plan benefits does not necessarily mean that you have been terminated from your job.

As a practical matter, the easiest thing for you to do would be to simply call or write your employer and ask for clarification of your job status. Ask them about the reason for the termination of your pension/profit-sharing plan. If they fail to respond, send them a certified letter asking for your lawful right to inspect your employee file. Perhaps the file will contain documentation answering your questions.

77

EMPLOYMENT STATUS COMPLAINTS

Status as Independent Contractor in Question

Q I am a home care worker who works for various agencies in my area. One agency has me on its payroll as an employee. It takes care of my withholding, contributes to my social security and provides other benefits such as workers' compensation and unemployment insurance. Another agency treats me as an independent contractor and does not contribute to my Social Security or workers' comp.

Both agencies call me with assignments to work in the community for people who have health problems and need some home care. Both tell me which days I am to work and what hours. Both agencies also collect from the family members and then turn around and pay me. Is it legal for one agency to treat me as an independent contractor?

—D. D., Irvine

A How an employer classifies its workers, either as employees or independent contractors, can have severe consequences. Employers can be assessed massive penalties, liabilities and even possibly criminal charges for misclassifying workers.

Employees who are misclassified may unnecessarily be liable for increased taxes, lose insurance coverage, and incur liabilities to third parties.

Yet, despite these problems, employers continue to misclassify their workers as independent contractors. This may be understandable because the test for an independent contractor is by no means clear. In fact there are several different types of tests that are used, depending upon which government entity or other party is evaluating the employment status. Most states and many government agencies use a six factor list:

·Control.
·Opportunities for profit or loss depending on a worker's managerial skill.
·Investment in facilities or employment of helpers.
·Need for special skills.
·Permanent relationship.
·Integration into alleged employer's business.

As a home care worker, it appears that you should be classified as an employee rather than an independent contractor. It is actually possible for you to be an employee for one agency and an independent contractor for the other, though it does not seem likely. One agency may not have as much control over you, give you as much discretion, require your purchase and use of expensive tools or equipment, insist upon special skills or training and consider you as an integral part of the their business as the other agency.

If you complain to the agency that has perhaps misclassified you as an independent contractor and you are terminated, you may have a wrongful termination claim as a whistle-blower. I suggest that you make the request in writing in a diplomatic manner.

It is illegal for an employer to retaliate against an employee who complains about an illegality or violation of a "fundamental public policy" based in law or the Constitution.

SLANDER

78

LIES ABOUT YOU

Slander Is Illegal

Q I worked for a marketing company for almost 1½ years in both management and as a research analyst catering to high-tech clients. I was the object of untruthful, malicious, behind-the-back slander by another supervisor.

Fellow employees would tell me that on my sick days this supervisor would have floor meetings and publicly blame me for things that were not my responsibility or could be attributable directly to his incompetence.

I was fired one day in December while I was out sick because, during a client-management telephone conference, I was blamed by company management for carrying out directions that the client found didn't meet their needs.

Is there recourse against this supervisor or the company? Many employees have told me they would testify about the things that occurred behind my back. My work record was perfect. I never received a warning for poor work or any complaint to my face for any work habit or quality.

—S.D., Woodland Hills

A If you were humiliated or your performance other-wise suffered because of these untruthful statements, you could have a legal claim against your co-worker, since slander is illegal. What you could obtain from that claim would have to be determined.

You should be able to show that the lies resulted, at least in part, in your termination. However, the company would probably contend that there was no connection between the untruthful statements and its claim that you were not meeting the needs of your client.

Evaluate your employee hand-book to determine if the employer has a progressive discipline system.

There is no legal requirement that your employer warn you before termination. Since you only worked at the company 1½ years, you are probably classified as an "at-will" employee who could be terminated with or without a good reason.

Evaluate your employee handbook to determine if the employer has a progressive discipline system. Certainly, they need to comply with any promises to give warnings or have sufficient cause prior to termination.

79

SLANDER BY SUPERVISORS

There Are Limits to
Criticism in the Office

Q I work for a very large corporation. At our local office we have three immediate supervisors, and two of them are making the employees' work life very stressful to the point it is almost unbearable. They continuously make derogatory remarks about employees to other employees, threaten employees with their jobs and make derogatory remarks against the third supervisor to other employees. They fly off the handle, refusing to talk with employees for days if they feel like it. They discuss people's job performances with other employees rather than in private.

Numerous employees have complained over and over about these two supervisors. The supervisors in the past have been reprimanded, but that was as far as it went. Do we, as employees, have to be subjected to this kind of verbal abuse and unprofessional treatment? Where can we obtain any publications for employee rights in the workplace?

—N.N., Long Beach

A Slander in the workplace is often a big problem. Employers will argue that varying types of management styles are permitted. Supervisors need to comment about workplace situations to the employees involved and others as well to make a point. They will characterize the derogatory remarks as constructive criticism to improve performance.

On the other hand, employees can also argue that such improper remarks go beyond the privilege of private discussion among management. This is especially true if the remarks are false. The employee handbook might even regulate the manner in which comments about performance are to be made. The comments might even violate the company's promise of fairness and sensitivity towards employment issues.

The law allows certain privileged communications within the workplace, especially among management and those with a "need to know." Those who are told, however, must have a justifiable reason to receive the information.

If the remarks are untruthful, an employee might have a claim for slander. On the other hand, if the remarks are truthful but are simply poor management style, violate company policy or are harassing in nature based upon discrimination, the employer may also be liable.

If the employer knows about an impropriety in the workplace and fails to correct it, I suggest you write about your complaints to higher management. Review the rules of your own company. If you don't have a handbook, or you are unsure of the policy, check with your human resources department. If the treatment is discriminatory against you, based on age, sex, race or any other recognized basis, your case would be much stronger than if the supervisor is simply a harasser of all groups.

In the alternative, consider sending a letter to the harassing supervisors directly before going over their heads. They might appreciate the consideration, which might lessen the chance of retaliation.

80

PERSONNEL FILE LIES

Lies in Personnel Files?
How Much Is the Truth Worth?

Q My employer keeps a personnel file on each employee. The policy is not to show it unless an individual asks to see it.

I had never asked to see it in my 13 years at the company and when I did it was full of innuendoes, misrepresentations and outright lies. I feel I can prove them to be lies.

Should I take it to upper management or go outside the company to handle this situation? I am a union member.

—J.T., Fullerton

A There is no doubt that misrepresentation in your personnel file can drastically affect your future with your employer. You should decide if you should correct the problem before you decide how to do it. It appears interesting that you are even still there after 13 years if these comments about you are so harmful.

Evaluate your own job security. Would complaining make the situation worse? If you are six months away from retirement, you may want to do nothing.

Evaluate the harm of these lies to you and whether action will change anything. If there is very little management personnel over you, and if you will remain under the same manager after complaining about this, would it really do any good? Sure, you might get it removed from your file, but it may never really change the attitude of the person who put it there. In fact, it may even cause your relations to worsen.

It is illegal to defame another person. In the last few years, however, there have been several cases that have limited certain types of defamation claims in the workplace by calling it "privileged communication" between members of management. Some cases have limited defamation rights even when a personnel file is involved.

You are certainly justified in reviewing all of your options, however, and acting on them when your good character has been tarnished.

You may have many rights under the company's own policy or your union contract. You should review them both. Despite some limitations, you may have rights to have lies about you removed from your personnel file, or prevent them from happening in the future.

You should follow any grievance procedure established by your company or union contract. You could send a rebuttal letter to management and ask them to place it in your file for future reference. A letter from an attorney informing the company of the law of defamation might accomplish much.

You should also consider the reason why such information was placed in your file. If a supervisor's motive was based in any way upon discrimination or retaliation against you for being a whistle-blower, then your rights might expand to include other important charges besides the defamation.

The employee handbook might even regulate the manner in which comments about performance are to be made.

PRIVACY

81

PRIVACY RIGHTS

Worker Privacy Can't Be Invaded Unreasonably

Q A friend of mine was recently hired by a company that is not based in the United States. One of the items on the employment agreement says that while employed by the company, you will not, except with the written consent of the company, devote any of your time to any other business or profession.

I can understand where they would not want you to be in a competing business, but if you have some other part-time venture that does not infringe on the company's interests, how could that item be enforceable?

—V.C., Mission Viejo

A A company cannot unreasonably invade the privacy of its employees. Companies not based in the United States must also comply with U.S. law in this regard.

The courts have held that companies can prohibit

employees from engaging in outside employment that is in competition with its own business. If the outside employment is not in competition with the company's business then there must be some other legitimate reason for the restriction for it to be legally enforceable. If an employee is a part-time employee, it would be very difficult to justify any restriction on outside non-competitive employment.

The key is whether or not the outside employment unreasonably affects the work performance or other relevant factors within the company. Some of the factors that would have to be evaluated on a case-by-case basis include the following: effect on employee absenteeism, harm to the company's reputation (especially if the outside employment is disreputable or illegal), and the extent to which other employees fear or refuse to work with the employee because of outside employment or activities.

Unfortunately, employers sometimes put provisions in employment agreements or employee handbooks that have the legal effect of an unenforceable suggestion. Your friend may have a legal claim against his employer if he is fired or suffers retaliation because of his refusal to submit to unreasonable intrusions into his private life.

On the other hand, rather than complaining about an unjust policy and possibly suffering retaliation or fighting a battle over the problem, he might be better off by simply keeping his outside employment quiet and dealing with the improper policy if the employer discovers his violation of it.

> *Companies can prohibit employees from engaging in outside employment that is in competition with its own business. The key is whether the outside employment unreasonably affects the work performance or other relevant factors within the company.*

82
IMPROPER QUESTIONS

*There Are Some Things Employers
Can't Ask*

Q When a job applicant is providing information, is an employer allowed to ask whether he has ever filed for unemployment?

—A.R., Los Angeles

A A variety of laws restrict employers from asking certain questions in the hiring process. Questions that even hint at a discriminatory bias of the employer or violate certain rights of privacy are inappropriate, for example. Inquiries that identify an applicant's sex, age, race, color, national origin, ancestry, marital status, religion, physical handicap, or medical condition are prohibited.

Questions on whether an applicant has ever been arrested or filed workers' compensation benefits are prohibited by statute. Along the same line, it is probably inappropriate to ask applicants whether they have filed a discrimination complaint with the Equal Employment Opportunity Commission or filed for unemployment compensation. These are rights given to you by law.

Perhaps the employer wants to find out if you have a propensity for losing jobs or filing for unemployment, which might have a financial impact on them. An employer certainly can ask you about your job history. But even though there are no specific laws against it, an employer probably has crossed the line if he asks about unemployment compensation.

A variety of laws restrict employers from asking certain questions in the hiring process. Questions that even hint at a discriminatory bias are inappropriate.

The problem with refusing to answer any question on a job interview is that it might prevent you from getting the job. If that happens and you feel you were more qualified than the successful applicant, you might have a claim against the company.

It would be useful to get the names and phone numbers of other applicants prior to the interview, so that you could talk with them to determine if they had been asked the same questions. That way it would not be just your word against your prospective employer's.

83

DRUGS

*Employee's Drug Use Is Bringing
Quality, Morale Down*

Q An employee at the manufacturing company I work for uses drugs on the job frequently. Although management is aware of the problem, they do not approach him because he is the brother of the production manager.

His drug use is affecting his work. Because he is important to the production process, quality also is affected. Yet management blames the whole department for the low quality. I don't know how to begin going about this problem.

—D.R., La Habra

A It certainly seems unfair to blame the whole department for the substandard work of one employee who is on drugs. There is an obvious double standard in the workplace.

You might begin by reviewing your company's own policy regarding drugs. Read the employee handbook or other written policy statements. Determine if the employer has violated its own stated rules. This will help establish your claim for breach of contract.

Consider safety issues. Does the employee on drugs present a hazard to other workers or ultimately to the consumer of substandard products? Research if the employee's drug use is, in fact, illegal. Is this an occasional use of mild drugs or blatant addiction to illegal hard drugs? Is the use something for which this employee could be arrested and convicted of a crime?

You have a number of options. You could submit confidential correspondence to the human resources department regarding the problem. You could divulge your own name in a complaint after asking for privacy. If privacy is breached, you may have a claim against the company for the damages you incur.

Complaining about a safety issue, illegalities or discrimination in the workplace is a protected activity.

A letter could be written in a very positive manner, if the main point is increasing production, not particularly attacking the other employee. Out of courtesy, you could direct the letter confidentially only to the production manager. If the problem is not resolved to your satisfaction, you could go to the next level of management. As an alternative you could totally avoid the production manager by going over his head to the owner and request confidentiality.

As a last option, even though it is a very severe one, you could complain to the police department and actually have the other worker arrested. Although it will obviously not endear you to his brother, the production manager, you will be legally protected from retaliation.

Complaining about a safety issue in the workplace, illegalities or discrimination in the workplace is a protected activity. If you are retaliated against because of these actions, you will have a valid claim against your employer.

84

I.Q. TESTS

Test May Violate
Privacy Law

Q After a job interview, I was asked to come back for a test. The interviewer did not say what the test would be. It turned out to be a battery of psychological tests and what I believe was an IQ test.

I was never offered a job, and I'm now bothered that this company has highly personal information about me. It also bothers me that they did not gain my informed consent to take these tests.

Do I have a right to the originals of these tests? How should I approach the company?

—L. D., San Diego

A A psychological or intelligence test may violate privacy and discrimination laws. These tests sometimes ask very subtle questions to gain information about religious, political or sexual beliefs of the applicant. Such motives may not be readily apparent on the surface. It would certainly be easier to evaluate the legality of such a test if you could obtain a copy of it.

Although you may have an argument that the company violated your privacy rights, this must be balanced against the interests of the employer to obtain certain information on a reasonable basis. You have to consider the type of job for which you were applying. Jobs requiring certain physical or mental skills might justify questions that would otherwise constitute an invasion of privacy.

Privacy rights must be balanced against the interests of the employer to obtain certain information on a reasonable basis. Jobs requiring certain skills might justify questions that would otherwise constitute an invasion of privacy.

Even though you objected to these tests, it may be difficult to prove a connection between the results of the tests and the fact that you did not get the job. If possible, compare your qualifications with those of the person who eventually got the job.

You have a right to inspect these tests and to get a copy, although the company is entitled to keep the original. You can certainly ask the company to give you the original and all the copies of the test since you did not get the job. If they refuse, demand that they keep the results strictly confidential.

85

PSYCHOLOGICAL TESTS

Psychological Tests Must Be Kept Private

Q My employer put me on leave and required me to take a psychological examination after I had a heated confrontation with my supervisor while grieving a reprimand. After the exam, I was told the results were normal and that I could report back to work. About two weeks later, I found out that my employer had received a written report of the psychological/fitness exam and that it contained personal information about me and my immediate family.

Now I'm concerned about how my employer might use this information. Did the company violate my right to privacy? Can I force my employer to remove the report from its internal files? Are there any restrictions on how the company can use this information?

—R.S., Los Angeles

A Under certain circumstances, employers may require employees to take a psychological examination. Certainly they have a duty to prevent violence in the workplace. If the employer has reasonable cause to believe that you might be a threat to others, it can be legally required to pursue such an evaluation in good faith. The employer would have stronger justification if it has required such examinations of other employees as well.

Evaluate the need for the examination in the first place. Did your employer have reasonable justification based upon your actions? In the alternative, was it simply a harassment technique based on discrimination against you for another reason? Harassment or retaliation against you based on a discriminatory reason is strictly illegal.

Employers may require employees to take a psychological examination. Your employer must ensure the privacy of the results.

Your employer must ensure the privacy of the results. Otherwise, you may have a claim for invasion of privacy. Medical and psychological information should be kept strictly confidential.

You did not say, however, that your company has misused this information. Apparently, it simply received it from the physician. Your doctor/patient privacy rights may have been violated, but your claim might be more for medical malpractice rather than against your employer. Evaluate how the report got into the hands of your employer. Did your employer request it, or did the doctor unilaterally send it?

You certainly have a right to ask management to remove it from your file. It is illegal for them to rely upon this information if it is to your detriment. Unfortunately, if you make too big of an issue of removing the report from your file, management may remember the information much longer.

86
DRESS
CODE

Law Not Clear on
Men with Earrings on Job

Q I am a male supervisor who wears small hoop earrings (one in each ear). My company has no specific rules governing dress, but I have been pressured
to remove them. I've been told that it is not appropriate for a supervisor.

I don't think that the earrings impair my abilities
to supervise workers. What do you think?

—M.J., Anaheim

❖   ❖   ❖

A The answer to your actual question—whether earrings impair your abilities—is a subjective one
based on how the workers perceive you. Apparently,
your supervisor thinks that it affects your job.

Your legal rights are by no means clear. You could
certainly argue that you have a legal right to dress the

way you want. There are certain laws of privacy that restrict the ability of an employer to improperly regulate matters of a private concern. A current case established the right of a woman to wear pants to work, for example.

You might want to look at the employee handbook to see how much leeway they give you regarding this. Your position might be further justified depending upon the nature of work you do. For example, if the workers under you dress in a similar manner, your earrings might be appropriate.

If you deal with the public, the employer might be more justified in regulating dress and attire than if you do not.

Compare yourself with other supervisors to see if there is a double standard. Does your boss allow variations of dress and attire with other people in your same position, but not with you? You might have a discrimination claim.

On the other hand, the employer might argue that it has a legal interest to regulate attire and dress in the workplace. After all, Disneyland has withstood many legal challenges to its dress policy and has prevailed. If you deal with the public, the employer might be more justified in regulating dress and attire than if you do not. Complaints about your attire from those you supervise would give further justification to the employer's position.

"Looks" discrimination in employment is probably one of the most widespread areas of discrimination, and it becomes illegal only when you can link it to an established area of discrimination such as age, race, sex, breach of a contractual promise, or illegal retaliation, such as for whistle-blowing.

As a practical matter, evaluate how strongly you feel about keeping the earrings and weigh that against the risk that you might alienate your boss and affect your career stability.

87

PERSONNEL FILE EXCEPTIONS

City May Be Shielded from Personnel Law

Q I have worked for a small city in Orange County for more than two decades. During this time, I have taken several promotional exams. As part of this process, three higher-ranking personnel from other cities usually give an oral exam.

It has been the practice of my employer's personnel department to restrict the inspections of the "results," "notes," and/or "comments" by the examiners. The personnel department refuses to allow applicants to read the written material associated with their exam. They insist on reading it to the applicant. They claim files associated with promotional exams are not personnel files.

I believe I have the right to read the written results in their entirety, complete with the names of the examiners. Am I right?

—G.K., Buena Park

❖ ❖ ❖

A The Labor Code provides that employers must permit an employee to inspect any personnel file that is used or has been used to determine the employee's qualifications for employment, promotion, additional compensation, termination or other disciplinary action.

It would appear, according to this section and the cases interpreting it, that you have a right to review and read the results, notes and comments of the examiners on your exams. This right would only extend to your own file and not the exams of others.

The only problem is that public employers, as of 1993, became exempt from this law. It is possible that the city may have committed itself contractually in writing through the employee handbook or other documents to provide you with appropriate access to your file. Evaluate these documents.

> *An employer must permit an employee to inspect any personnel file used to determine the employee's qualifications for employment, promotion, termination or other disciplinary action.*

88

PERSONNEL FILE ACCESS

Each Worker Has the Right to Inspect Personnel File

Q I have a question about having access to my employee records. I asked my supervisor to look at my personnel file. At first she said that she could not let me review it, but that she could read it to me. Then she told me I had to go to our Personnel Department to look at it, which is at a separate location from where I work. My manager admits that she has a separate employee file on me, but was reluctant to show me. What are my rights to see all my employee files?

—J.D., Anaheim

A You have a statutory right to inspect your employee personnel file during reasonable business hours. You have a right to obtain a copy of any document which you have signed. You also are entitled to review other files which have been used to determine the conditions of your employment. Very often, an employer may keep a separate file other than your own file with other relevant documents in it. These are subject to your inspection as well. There have been cases of restricted access to supervisors' notes, however.

> *The very act of your confirming your own position by looking at your file might actually cause or influence what you are trying to prevent— job insecurity.*

In addition to the statutory rights, you might have a contractual right to a review of your file depending upon the promises of your employer, especially in the employee handbook.

Even if you cannot keep copies of it, consider taking notes of the relevant documents in the file, taking a picture of it with your own camera or dictating the contents of your file into your tape recorder.

Try to ask for it without any previous notice. The employer may allow you to see it without first reviewing it. Too much advance notice might allow them to "sanitize" the file to your detriment.

If they refuse you immediate access to your file, confirm your request in writing. This will help you later if they refuse your request.

The problem with asking for access to your file if you are still employed is that the employer might look at you suspiciously as trying to "position" yourself against the employer. This may hurt you later in more critical performance reviews in an effort of your employer to likewise position itself. The very act of your confirming your own position by looking at your file might actually cause or influence what you are trying to prevent—job insecurity.

89
POOR REVIEW OPTIONS

Disputing Your
Job Performance Review

Q If my employer has given me a negative review, what are the appropriate methods to dispute it, and their advantages and disadvantages?

—G.M., Mission Viejo

A Trying to justify any of your failures at the time of the review is too late. Frequent written communication to the boss throughout the year detailing your continuing plan of action and asking for input, which you follow, creates the favorable dilemma of linking any criticism of your performance with the boss's advice. Also, sign the review.

Too many employees refuse to sign a negative review, which usually only acknowledges receipt. Even if it doesn't, an employee can so condition the signature. Refusing to sign is often interpreted as insubordination and makes a bad situation worse.

Finally, don't try to win a battle that could cause you to lose the war. Carefully weigh the advantages of clearing up a negative review with the disadvantages of alienating or insulting your boss. If you, like most workers, can be fired at the will of the employer—with or without cause—then the most important review is not written but the subjective one in your boss's mind. If you contest your review, be diplomatic and respectful of a boss's often fragile ego.

> *Trying to justify any of your failures at the time of the review is too late. If you contest your review, be diplomatic and respectful of a boss's often fragile ego.*

90
BLACKLISTING

One Medical Mistake Shouldn't End Career

Q I recently lost my job with a respected medical organization. Throughout my employment, I regularly received praise and recognition from my supervisor for my performance. I had an exemplary history with my previous employer.

Unfortunately, I was dismissed because I inadvertently injected a patient with medication other than what was specified by the doctor on duty. Upon discovering this error, I immediately notified the doctor, who took corrective action. The medication was harmless and the patient did not suffer adverse side effects. The next day I was dismissed.

I am actively seeking employment and I feel that my previous employer will refer to this incident when prospective employers call for a reference, and will not emphasize my other professional skills and abilities. Although I recognize the significance of the incident, I don't think that my medical career should be ruined because of it. What can I do?

Also, can I still collect unemployment benefits even though I was discharged for this incident?

—R.P., Huntington Beach

A You have good reason to be concerned. Bad refer-ences can ruin a career.

Legally, a former employer can't blacklist you with other prospective employers. The problem here is that you may be more concerned that they are telling the truth rather than lying about you. If such statements are made, your former employer could defend itself by arguing there's a need to offer a truthful reference to fellow medical care providers. Employers would like to know, for example, if someone being considered for a job has been involved in repeated incidents of medical malpractice.

> *Legally, a former employer can't blacklist you with other prospective employers. Talk frankly with your past employer and get an agreement as to what they are going to say about you.*

But no employer wants to be sued, and a company realizes that its staff often says too much about a previous employee. I would suggest talking frankly with your past employer about your situation. Get an agreement as to what exactly they are going to say about you. Try to limit their references to confirming a basic description of your job and length of employment.

Consider having a friend call your former employer to check what they are saying about you. If it is a negative reference, write a letter warning that you may take legal action against them if it continues. For more impact, have an attorney write a letter.

In any case, you should get unemployment benefits because your termination did not stem from deliberate misconduct. You simply made a mistake.

*There are certain laws of privacy
that restrict the ability of an employer to
improperly regulate matters of a
private concern.*

UNEMPLOYMENT

91
MOONLIGHTING

Hourly Employee Told Not to Take
Second Job

Q As an hourly paid employee, does my employer have exclusive right to my services? I am told that I cannot work for another company, but I am having financial difficulty and need to work a part-time job.

—J.K., Thousand Oaks

❖   ❖   ❖

A What you do on your own time should not be the concern of your employer. You should be able to work part time after your regular daily work hours. Working another job on the weekend should be even less objectionable.

A ban on part-time work would appear to violate common rights of fairness, especially if this is a new policy after you have worked at the company many years.

On the other hand, some employers might have a legal right to make this demand. An employer can restrict your outside employment if it is with a competing company, for example.

You also may be in a job that requires erratic hours from day to day, or be available on a beeper-call system on your off hours.

Your employer might have a legitimate right to demand that you keep your schedule free of other work commitments. But if your freedom to do what you want to do on your off hours is limited, your employer may have to pay you for being on call.

> *Your rights might depend on whether or not this requirement was imposed on you from the first day of your employment, or unilaterally later on.*

Your employer's position is further justified if your work performance is affected because of other late-night work commitments.

Furthermore, your rights might depend on whether or not this requirement was imposed on you from the first day of your employment, or unilaterally later on. It doesn't sound like it is a definite written policy, but simply one that has been mentioned to you informally.

If you consider discreetly working another job and not telling your employer about it, realize you might get fired for doing it.

92

UNEMPLOYMENT COMPENSATION

Unemployment Compensation, Even If You Quit

Q I am planning on leaving my job. I can no longer stand the fabrications and embarrassing situations that the company president puts me in. He has trouble meeting the payroll from week to week and is not paying any of his current or past expenses. He has no ability to obtain any capital. He has already liquidated several items.

Basically, he should close shop and lay off the remaining employees, but he is being sued by the investors and doesn't want to accept defeat.

What are my chances of collecting unemployment if I quit? Can I lay myself off?

—H.B.

A You should have no problem collecting unemployment if you quit. The Employment Development Department will not hold your quitting against you when it is for such justifiable reasons as not receiving your wages, not receiving wages on time or intolerable conditions in the workplace.

A layoff occurs when the employer terminates your employment because of downsizing. That term should not be applied to your situation. You still should get your unemployment compensation whether your departure is called a layoff, quitting or being fired.

It may be important to document the conditions in the workplace before you end your employment. You might send your boss a letter documenting the nonpayment of wages, late payment of wages and other conditions. This may constitute appropriate proof in a subsequent application with the Employment Development Department for unemployment, or other actions that you might take.

It may be important to document the conditions in the workplace before you end your employment. The Employment Development Department will not hold quitting against you when it is for justifiable reasons.

Even though it appears the company itself is in great financial trouble, you still may have a claim against the company. The president may also be liable for the company's failure to pay your payroll taxes if it failed to do so.

The company and he may also be liable for penalties to the state for failure to pay wages in a timely manner. There may also be criminal penalties.

93

UNEMPLOYMENT COMPENSATION & RELOCATION

Loss of Unemployment Benefits for Refusal to Relocate

Q If your employer relocates out of state and the company offers you a job in the new location, but you refuse to move, can you still collect unemployment in California?

—D.T., Corona del Mar

A California Unemployment Insurance Code Section 1257 provides for disqualification for unemployment benefits if an employee refuses suitable employment without good cause. Although you do not give your reasons for refusing the offered employment, the inconvenience of relocating out of state would be good cause for refusing the employment.

If part of your reason for staying in California is because your spouse is employed here, then that would also qualify as good cause. Section 1256 states that voluntarily terminating employment to accompany a spouse to another state is good cause. The same would hold true if you were refusing to relocate to another state in order to stay with a spouse who is working in California.

California provides for disqualification for unemployment benefits if an employee refuses suitable employment without good cause. The distance of the employment from the employee's residence is taken into consideration when determining if employment is "suitable."

An additional question raised is whether the offer of employment in the new location qualifies as "suitable employment" under the code. Section 1258 states that the distance of the employment from the employee's residence is taken into consideration when determining if employment is "suitable." Since your employer has moved out of state, it is highly unlikely that you would be able to commute to the new job from your current residence, and therefore the employment would most likely not be determined to be suitable.

I recommend you contact your local Employment Development Department if you have any additional questions or you want assistance under the Displaced Worker Assistance program, which helps workers such as yourself who are out of a job because of their employer either going out of business or moving out of state as a result of the economy.

94

WORKERS' COMP. & UNEMPLOYMENT COMPENSATION

Job-Loss Benefits Sometimes Overlap

Q Can an employee who is injured on the job and receives workers' compensation also file for unemployment compensation? In other words, can he or she double dip? In New York state, that is permitted. Can an employee do that here?

—F.Z., La Habra

A To a certain extent, job-loss benefits do have overlapping benefits. For example, your own company may have a disability insurance plan that provides better coverage than what you might get through the workers' compensation system. Your workers' comp. benefits might offset to a degree the greater benefits received under the private plan.

Also, disability benefits you might receive under the state system in the event of injury do not analyze whether such injury happened during the course of your employment. Thus, if you are ineligible for payments under the workers' comp. program, you might get benefits through this other system. There are also different standards for Social Security benefits than for workers' comp.

> *To receive jobless benefits, you must be ready and able to work. To gain workers' comp., you need to show just the opposite.*

In regard to unemployment compensation, the rule is "either one or the other." To receive jobless benefits, you must be able to show that you are ready and able to work. To gain compensation under the workers' comp. rules, you need to show just the opposite. Some people file under both systems and let the state figure it out. In the event one system says you are ineligible, then you would receive benefits from the other.

You may receive compensation through one of the governmental systems and also through a private claim. The reasons behind the job injury or job loss must be evaluated. If those reasons include discrimination or retaliation for complaining about some illegality or slander, you might have an additional basis to recover more money than would be provided by governmental benefits. In fact, those other claims might not only compensate you for your wage loss but also give you the equivalent of punitive damages because of wrongful acts by your employer.

95

UNEMPLOYMENT COMPENSATION AFTER RESIGNATION

A Vow to Resign Might Be Irrevocable

Q I worked for a government agency, which has approved my voluntary resignation, including a bonus, on a certain date. The document states that this action is irrevocable.

Now my financial status has changed, and I want to withdraw my resignation, which doesn't take effect for a couple of months. The agency responded in writing that my resignation was irrevocable and I will still be forced to resign, maybe this time without a bonus.

What recourse do I have against the government, my employer? Since I sought to withdraw the resignation, would my voluntary resignation be reclassified a firing, therefore qualifying me for unemployment insurance after I depart?

—Y.T., Calabasas

A "Promises are promises," your employer will argue. Just as you expect them to abide by their contractual commitments, so do they expect you to comply with your resignation. There is no wiggling out, they will claim.

You could try arguing that you have caused them no harm. Perhaps they have not even found your replacement yet. In the end, they will probably prevail with their argument. You simply resigned and they accepted that resignation. It is a contract.

I don't understand why they are now threatening to withdraw the bonus. If they argue that your resignation and their acceptance of it was an irrevocable contract, their promise to pay you a bonus should be the same.

You might ultimately get unemployment insurance even though you resigned. You could argue that you tried to cancel the resignation and caused the employer no harm.

You might ultimately get unemployment insurance even though you resigned. If they argue that your resignation and their acceptance of it was an irrevocable contract, their promise to pay you a bonus should be the same.

You could argue that your reason for resigning was justifiable. For example, if you took this action because of discrimination or other illegal actions in the workplace, it will be deemed as a "constructive termination," entitling you to unemployment benefits.

Job-loss benefits may overlap.

RECOURSE

96
SUE YOUR EMPLOYER?

Don't Be Hasty in Filing
a Lawsuit

Q If my attorney has encouraged me to sue my former employer, what are the advantages and disadvantages of trying to solve an employment dispute through litigation?

—J.P., Laguna Hills

A My response to clients whose first reaction to an employment dispute is to file a lawsuit is, "Not so fast." There are numerous ways to resolve such a dispute, including negotiation by yourself or an attorney, an employer's internal grievance procedure, mediation, arbitration or other private settlement services, and help from an appropriate government agency. Which of these methods is best depends on how you evaluate the option of litigation.

Usually, it isn't just a question of suing or not suing but an evaluation of whether you could obtain your minimum demands through other, easier means.

Usually, it isn't just a question of suing or not suing but an evaluation of whether you could obtain your minimum demands through other, easier means.

Before deciding to sue, consider these factors: emotional stress, your financial needs now and in the future, the future value of a lower money settlement now and the tax consequences, the value of your lost time, possible publicity about your case, attorney fees and other expenses of litigation, the future availability of witnesses, unforeseen changes in the law, your ability to collect a judgment, the effect a lawsuit could have on your credit rating and future job prospects and, of course, the risk of defeat. Think carefully before determining whether to seek a settlement or to sue a former employer. Selecting litigation may drastically change your financial and emotional health.

97

AGENCY OR ATTORNEY HELP

Resolving Employment Disputes:
Government Agencies vs. Attorneys

Q If one has a variety of employment claims, what are the advantages and disadvantages of seeking help through a government agency, as compared to an attorney?

— S.M., Laguna Niguel

A The main government agencies that handle employment disputes, such as the state's Labor Commissioner Office, Department of Fair Employment and Housing, the U.S. Department of Labor or U.S. Equal Employment Opportunity Commission, often are very helpful in resolving employment discrimination, whistle-blower or wage disputes. The biggest advantage is that they are free.

The agencies' clerical workers may even have more specialized knowledge on various types of employment disputes than a generalist attorney. In some circumstances, filing with a government agency may even extend a statute of limitations deadline.

The problem is that government agencies are often very slow. It may take up to a year to begin an investigation. They are underbudgeted and understaffed, and as a result it is difficult for them to give much personalized service. The clerical staff, who are not lawyers, may not give complete legal advice as to all potential employment claims. Each agency seems to have blinders that limit it to handle only its own particular type of dispute, but not others. None of the agencies handle certain types of employment claims, such as fraud, slander or breach of contract, which can only be handled by an attorney.

The biggest advantage of government agencies is that they are free. Attorneys help by evaluating and pursuing all potential employment claims.

Attorneys help resolve employment disputes by evaluating and pursuing all potential employment claims. Accordingly, they may be perceived as a bigger threat to an employer than a government agency would for a limited claim.

The biggest problem with attorneys is their cost. Some attorneys may charge on an hourly basis with no limit.

Others may charge on a contingent fee, in which there is no fee unless there is a recovery. Some attorneys have a combination of the two with a small retainer up-front.

Another disadvantage may be in receiving advice from an attorney who may not have complete knowledge of this area of law. The best solution may be to initially consult with a specialist attorney—on a limited fee basis—on all possible claims and how to use, if needed, the cheaper government agencies to one's best benefit.

98
WAGE CLAIM THROUGH STATE AGENCY

Claim for Back Wages Stalls in State Agency

Q In 1995 I filed a complaint with the Department of Labor Standards Enforcement, claiming my former employer owed me more than $60,000.

My former employer did not pay me back wages, overtime, vacation pay, expense money, profit sharing or bonuses going back to 1994. They even kept my 401(k) money.

The company is still in business, earning record profits, and even sent the labor standards department part of the money owed. But the department returned the money to the company without notifying me. Now the department has refused my phone calls and has not answered my letters.

Please let me know what I can do to put my case back on track.

—J.P., Brea

AEven though the Division of Labor Standards Enforcement (the Labor Commissioner's office) is underbudgeted and overworked, it makes no sense whatsoever for them to return money to the company and to refuse your calls. Since your case is relatively old, arising in 1995, we wonder if you failed to properly inform the department of your current address.

Consider asking to talk to the senior deputy at their office, or going to the office and asking to inspect your file over the counter. Determine whether your case is still open. You have three years to pursue your wage claims from the time they arose.

An attorney might be able to help you get action out of the Labor Commissioner's office. Your 401(k) money is yours, not the employer's. Pursuing your claim through the Division of Labor Standards Enforcement is not your only option. You could always file an independent lawsuit against your employer.

> *Pursuing your claim through the Division of Labor Standards Enforcement is not your only option. You could always file a lawsuit against your employer.*

99

RECOURSE FOR VIOLENCE

Employers Required to Guard Against Workplace Violence

Q Recently a threat was made upon my life by a co-worker. I told my supervisor, but it took a long time for management to acknowledge the threat. This co-worker had a knife in his drawer, and has done nothing but cause unpleasantness at work. They called him in and changed his hours, kind of slapped him on the hand, and said you can't do that. Legally, I don't know what I can do. I'm afraid if I say anything, I'll lose my job.

—M., Buena Park

A The employer has an absolute obligation to provide a safe workplace. Management should act promptly to investigate any complaint of violence and take appropriate steps to prevent it in the future.

You should complain in writing to management if you are still fearful of the other employee. You could demand that he be terminated. It is illegal for the employer to retaliate against you because you reasonably complain about a workplace safety situation.

I have counseled employees who have been injured or who have injured others in the workplace, and have talked to relatives of those who have been killed.

Based on those discussions, here are some sugges-
tions:

• Internal grievance procedure. The employer should
have adequate procedures by which employees can
complain about perceived violence or threats of violence.

• Appropriate investigation. Employers should investigate any complaint regarding another employee.
During the hiring process, employers should evaluate
an employee's propensity for violence. Employers
should warn employees in writing that management
has the right to search drawers and lockers to find
company property or to insure safety in the workplace.

• Discipline Procedure. Termination of employment is
certainly an option for serious offenses. An employer
could consider calling the police for a serious crime,
such as a threat against the life of another employee.

• Education. Management personnel should be
trained in how to prevent violence in the workplace. By
state law, employers are to have a safety program and
to advise employees of it.

• Fairness with employees. If the employer would avoid
any hint of discrimination, improper retaliation or
other acts of unfairness, many problems would be prevented.

• Awareness. Management and workers need to be
aware of the significant signs of stress or irritability
that might lead to violence.

• Fairness with customers. Many acts of violence are
caused by disgruntled customers. A supervisor or
manager should become involved to show the customer that they are being taken seriously and with
compassion and understanding.

• Feedback. Violent actions often occur because a termination or demotion was unexpected. Annual performance reviews or other methods to give employees
feedback about job performance would lessen the sud-
den impact and surprise that comes with such
actions.

100

UNION

RECOURSE

Union v. Non-Union Employee Involvement

Q I am a transferee registered nurse to an affiliate hospital-medical clinic. My job seniority is five years, but my total years of service to this HMO is 10 years.

Last September, the management announced a reduction in force. My clinic job as a pediatric nurse is on the line. Before the realignment, officers of my union, the United Nurses Association of California, promised me in front of witnesses that they would upgrade my seniority date to compensate for my 10 years of total service. By doing that, I wouldn't have to bid for one of the remaining positions.

On the day of my job bidding, the union did not upgrade my seniority as promised. I was then forced to bid on the part-time job position.

I recently found out that two years ago there were job cuts among the hospital nurses and some were given credit for seniority to compensate for their years of service.

I feel betrayed by my union. Is it legal for the union to do this to me? Can I take legal action?

—L.C., Corona

Whenever a union is involved, the employee's claim for breach of contract is against the union and not the employer. You have an employment contract through your union and the union has a contract with the employer. The union is your sole bargaining agent in regard to contractual matters.

You may have a claim for breach of contract. It appears that you can prove through your witnesses that the promise was made. You relied upon their promises by continuing to work up to the date of the reduction in force.

Whenever a union is involved, the employee's claim for breach of contract is against the union and not the employer.

On the other hand, the union might argue that there is no "consideration" or bargain coming from your direction that makes it into a binding promise. They might argue that it was just their "intention" but not a contractual promise. Other factors may have influenced them to not fulfill the terms of their anticipated, but not definitely promised, actions.

Some union contracts have extremely short periods in which you must make the claim, even as short as a matter of days. You should review your union contract to see what the rules are in that regard.

It is interesting that they allowed such changes of status in the past to other nurses. You should evaluate why they did it to them and not to you now. If the difference in treatment is in any way related to discrimination or retaliation against you because you complained about any illegalities, you might have additional claims against the union.

As a practical consideration, weigh the advantages of fighting your union and what you hope to gain against the disadvantages of them possibly black-listing you in the future. I have had many clients who have tried to win a small battle presently, but lose a bigger war later.

101

DEMOTION

OPTIONS

Qualifications Are Key in Wrongful-Demotion Claim

Q I have been employed by a very large health-care company for five years. Two years into my employment as a vice president's secretary, my boss was promoted to our main office in Chicago. After eight months of teaching his successor the ropes, he called me into his office to tell me that I would be demoted and that a secretary, new to the organization, was to take my job.

He gave me no explanation for the decision other than he wanted the other secretary. I checked with the human resources manager and was told: "He can do whatever he wants."

Since that time there has been a reorganization. Both my boss and the human resources manager were laid off and the replacement secretary quit.

As a result of the demotion, I did not get a pay cut, but the salary framework for my level has prohibited any raises for the last two years. There is nothing in my file regarding the demotion other than the paperwork to make the change in jobs. My performance review is "outstanding." Do I have grounds to take legal action?

—S.L., Fountain Valley

A You may have a claim for "wrongful demotion." The key is to understand the real reason for the demotion. Compare yourself with your replacement. Was the new secretary more qualified? If not, were there any differences between you and her based on age, race, sex or other type of discrimination? What promises were made to you by management or the employee handbook regarding seniority and demotions? These questions need to be answered to fully evaluate your rights.

It is improper for management to demote you based on discrimination or retaliation against you for an improper purpose. Also, they need to abide by any contractual promises with you.

It appears, however, that your damages may be very limited because of the action. Apparently, there has been a reorganization and your superior was laid off. It is unclear whether your replacement quit on her own accord or because of an impending layoff.

If your old job no longer exists, they may have actually done you a favor by giving you this other job. Even though your job prohibited raises in the last two years, it appears that it was simply based on your level of employment rather than being discriminatory against you individually.

Since more than two years have passed, many of your claims might have expired because of your delays. Claims based on discrimination probably expired after a year. Claims for breach of oral contract might have expired after two years. Other claims might still exist, however.

You also can still complain about the situation. I would suggest you do your homework first and evaluate other jobs outside your company. You might find that your current job position, although a demotion from your former one, earns you more money than other comparable jobs on the outside.

There are numerous ways to resolve a dispute.

APPENDIX

APPENDIX A

Free Government Help on Discrimination Claims

There are two main government agencies which help in pursuing claims of discrimination in the workplace. The California Department of Fair Employment and Housing (DFEH) and the federal Equal Employment Opportunity Commission (EEOC) investigate complaints of harassment or discrimination in employment based on race, color, ancestry, religious creed, sex, disability (including AIDS and HIV), national origin, age (40+), pregnancy, medical condition and denial of medical care, family care or pregnancy disability leave. The DFEH also investigates discrimination claims based on marital status and medical conditions. Employers are prohibited from taking any retaliatory action against employees who file a complaint. The decision of which agency should help in pursuing a claim is an important one.

Filing Requirements

In order for these agencies to enforce these laws, certain conditions must apply. The DFEH accepts claims from all employees except those in unions and workers in the federal government. The EEOC accepts claims from all employees, except for those with disability discrimination claims against federal employers. For DFEH claims, employers must have at least one employee for a harassment claim and five employees for a discrimination claim. Both agencies require that employers have 50 employees for a Family Medical Leave Act claim. The EEOC requires that employers have a minimum of 15 employees for all claims except age discrimination claims, which require 20 employees, and claims against government entities, which require 25 employees.

Deadline for Filing with Agency

Both agencies impose deadlines by which date a claim must be filed to entitle an employee to pursue rights based on these laws. DFEH claims must be filed within one year of the wrongful act. EEOC claims have a 300-day deadline. Both agencies usually cross-file with each other to give complainants protection under both federal and state laws.

Deadline for Filing in Court

After an investigation and issuance of a "Right to Sue" letter, a lawsuit must be filed to pursue rights based on these laws within 90 days for EEOC claims and one year for DFEH claims.

Advantages of Both Agencies

Use of these agencies to enforce employee rights is free. The information they obtain can be used at trial even if they close the file. It puts pressure on the employers to pay money or reinstate a job. It extends the statute of limitations deadlines for discrimination claims. An employee must file with the appropriate agency before filing a lawsuit for claims based on these laws.

Advantages of the DFEH

Most employee rights attorneys prefer the DFEH over the EEOC because it enforces more discrimination laws, applies to more employers, is quicker (about one year instead of two years), has rules which make claims easier to prove, provides for more enforcement in administrative hearings before litigation, is not as limited on monetary recoveries, is more convenient with almost four times as many offices, and has a longer filing period to file with them or the court.

Advantages of the EEOC

The EEOC may be preferred over the DFEH on certain cases because it allows an out-of-state case to be conveniently filed locally, has possible broader coverage or recourse on certain cases, takes longer to investigate (which may be preferred by one who wants the delay for personal reasons), is more likely to pursue a class action claim and may be the only choice because of the nature of the claim, location of the employer or refusal of DFEH to accept a case.

Disadvantages of Both Agencies

Because of budget constraints, the agencies cannot provide as timely or thorough an investigation or prosecution of rights as might be desired. A finding of insufficient evidence of discrimination may harm an employee's ability to resolve the claim by settlement or litigation later. An investigation may cause other claims of an employee to expire by the delay. The agencies only handle those narrow issues within their jurisdiction. There are many other discrimination laws which provide protection that are not covered by these agencies. If an employee has other potential claims, the agency will not explore or identify them. An employee may want to consult an attorney who will expeditiously pursue all potential claims.

Department of Fair Employment and Housing Offices
(800) 884-1684

Bakersfield
1001 Tower Way, #250
Bakersfield, CA 93309-1586
(805) 395-2729

Fresno
1320 East Shaw, # 150
Fresno, CA 93710
(559) 244-4760

San Diego
350 West Ash Street, #950
San Diego, CA 92101-3901
(619) 645-2681

San Francisco
455 Golden Gate Ave., #7600
San Francisco, CA 94102-6073
(415) 703-4177

Los Angeles
611 West 6th St., #1500
Los Angeles, CA 90017
(213) 439-6700

Oakland
1515 Clay St., #701
Oakland, CA 94612-2512
(510) 622-2941

Sacramento
2000 "O" Street, #120
Sacramento, CA 95814-5212
(916) 445-5523

San Bernardino
1845 S. Business Center Dr.
#127
San Bernardino, CA 92408-3426
(909) 383-4373

San Jose
111 North Market St., #180
San Jose, CA 95113-1102
(408) 277-1271

Santa Ana
28 Civic Center Drive, #200
Santa Ana, CA 92701-4010
(714) 558-4266
(800) 884-1684
(800) 700-2320

Ventura
1732 Palma Dr., #200
Ventura, CA 93003
(805) 654-4514

Equal Employment Opportunity Commission Offices

Los Angeles
255 East Temple, 4th Fl.
Los Angeles, CA 90012
(213) 894-1000
(213) 894-1121

Fresno
1265 W. Shaw Ave.,#103
Fresno, CA 93711
(209) 487-5793
(209) 487-5837

San Francisco
901 Market Street, #500
San Francisco, CA 94103
(415) 356-5100
(415) 356-5098

Oakland
1301 Clay Street
Oakland, CA 94612-5217
(510) 637-3230
(510) 637-3234

San Jose
96 N. 3rd St., #200
San Jose, CA 95112
(408) 291-7352
(408) 291-7374

San Diego
401 "B" St., #1550
San Diego, CA 92101
(619) 557-7235
(619) 557-7232

APPENDIX B

Free Government Help on Wage & Working Condition Claims

The California Division of Labor Standards Enforcement (DLSE) is under the direction of the California State Labor Commissioner. The U.S. Department of Labor (DOL) and the Wage and Hour Division of the DSLE enforce laws on wages and working conditions. They also enforce prohibitions on retaliation against employees who file claims with them.

Filing Requirements

Almost all employees are entitled to file these claims. The DLSE has no jurisdiction over claims of construction and government workers. Independent contractors are not deemed employees. An employee should keep records (calendars, timecards) of any overtime to provide to the agency to help prove the claim.

Deadline for Filing Claims

From the date of the violation of the law, DLSE claims must be filed within 30 days for retaliation, two years for breach of oral contract, three years for overtime and four years for written contract. DOL claims must be filed within two years.

Advantages of Both Agencies

Use of these agencies to enforce employee rights is free. It puts pressure on the employer to settle the dispute. It extends the statute of limitations deadlines for discrimination claims.

Advantages of the DSLE

California laws usually have broader protection for workers. The DLSE enforces mandatory paid ten minute breaks for every four hours during a shift, mandatory meal breaks (unpaid), sick leave, vacation and other benefits. The DOL does not enforce any of these rights. In March of 1998, California increased its minimum wage to $5.75 an hour, whereas the federal minimum wage is only $5.15 per hour. The DLSE also allows more employees to be eligible for overtime pay. The DLSE is more likely to pursue individual claims. The DOL prefers to pursue actions which involve several employees against one employer.

Advantages of DOL

The DOL has stricter child labor laws. The DOL also may enforce oral wage agreements between employers and agricultural workers, whereas the DLSE only enforces minimum wages. In addition, construction and government employees can pursue their claims with the DOL. Currently, claims are processed more quickly with the DOL than with the DLSE.

Disadvantages of Both Agencies

Budgetary constraints prevent the agencies from providing as quick and complete a service as might be desired. A finding that there is insufficient evidence may harm the ability of an employee to later attempt to resolve the claim by settlement or litigation. An investigation may cause other claims of an employee to expire by the delay. The agencies only handle those narrow issues within their jurisdiction. There are many other laws which provide protection that are not covered by these agencies. If an employee has other potential claims, the agency will not explore or identify them. An employee may want to consult an attorney who will expeditiously pursue all potential claims.

U.S. Department of Labor
Wage and Hour Division Offices

Bakersfield
3801 Pegasus Drive
Bakersfield, CA 93301
(661) 391-6185
FAX: (661) 391-6185

Fresno
906 "N" Street, Ste. 105
Fresno, CA 93721
(559) 487-5317
FAX: (559) 487-5497

Glendale
300 S. Glendale, Ste. 400
Glendale, CA 91205-5274
(818) 240-5274
(213) 894-6375
FAX: (213) 894-6845

Long Beach
501 W. Ocean Blvd,
Ste. 5100
Long Beach, CA 90802
(562) 980-32801
FAX: (562) 980-3283

Los Angeles
3660 Wilshire, Ste. 340
Los Angeles, CA 90010
(213) 252-7911
FAX: (213) 252-7726

Oakland
1301 Clay St., Ste. 1080N
Oakland, CA 94612
(510) 637-2949
FAX: (510) 637-2950

Ontario
3350 Shelby St., Ste. 340
Ontario, CA 91789
(909) 948-3594
FAX: (909) 948-1365

Oxnard
2530 Financial Sqr., Rm. 107
Oxnard, CA 93030
(805) 485-1121
FAX: (805) 485-1122

San Francisco
District Office
455 Market St., Ste. 800
San Francisco, CA 94105
(415) 744-5590
FAX: (415) 744-5088

San Jose
60 South Market St., Rm 420
San Jose, CA 95113
(408) 291-7730
FAX: (408) 291-7731

Santa Ana
34 Civic Center Dr., Rm. 402
P.O. Box 12950
Santa Ana, CA 92712
(714) 836-2156,7
FAX: (714) 836-2152

West Covina
100 N. Barranca, Ste. 850
West Covina, CA 91791
(626) 966-0478
FAX: (626) 966-5539

California Division of Labor Standards Enforcement Offices

Bakersfield
5555 California Ave.
Ste. 200
Bakersfield, CA 93309
(805) 395-2710

Eureka
619 Second St., Rm. 109
Eureka, CA 95501
(707) 445-9067

Fresno
770 E. Shaw Ave., Rm. 315
Fresno, CA 93710
(209) 248-8400

Long Beach
300 Oceangate, 3rd Floor
Long Beach, CA 90802
(213) 620-6330

Los Angeles
320 West 4th St.
Los Angeles, CA 90013
(213) 620-6330

Marysville
1204 E St.
Marysville, CA 95901
(916) 323-4920

Oakland
1515 Clay St., Ste. 801
Oakland, CA 94612
(415) 557-7878

Redding
2115 Akard Ave., Rm. 17
Redding, CA 96001
(916) 323-4920

Sacramento
2424 Arden Way, Ste. 360
Sacramento, CA 95825
(916) 323-4920

Salinas
1870 Main St., Ste. 150
Salinas, CA 93906
(415) 557-7878

San Bernardino
464 West 4th St., Rm. 348
San Bernardino, CA 92401
(909) 383-4334

San Diego
8765 Aero Drive, Ste. 125
San Diego, CA 92123
(619) 467-3002

San Francisco
P.O. Box 420603
San Francisco, CA 94142-3660
(415) 557-7878

San Jose
60 Rm. 120
San Jose, CA 95113
(415) 557-7878

Santa Ana

28 Civic Center Plaza
Rm. 625
Santa Ana, CA 92701
(213) 620-6330

Santa Barbara

411 E. Canon Perdido St.
Rm. 3
Santa Barbara, CA 93101
(805) 568-1222

Santa Rosa

50 D St., Ste. 360
Santa Rosa, CA 95404
(707) 445-9067

Stockton

31 E. Channel St., Rm. 317
Stockton, CA 95202
(209) 948-7770

Van Nuys

6150 Van Nuys Blvd.
Rm. 100
Van Nuys, CA 91401
(213) 620-6330

APPENDIX C

Free Government Help for the Unemployed

The Employment Development Department (EDD) Unemployment Insurance Program provides income when an employee becomes unemployed and is actively seeking other work. The EDD Disability Insurance Program pays benefits when an employee is physically or mentally unable to work due to a non-work-related disability. The Job Service Program provides free services such as job placement, employment counseling and job search workshops.

Employees
The services of EDD help almost all employees in California.

Employers
Almost all employers are required to pay unemployment insurance tax.

How to File an Unemployment Insurance Claim
Currently, the State of California EDD offices are switching over to a phone claim filing system. Call the EDD number listed in the white pages of your local phone book under "California, State of, Employment Development Department." A claimant should have the following information available when calling the EDD: Social Security number; the name, mailing address and zip code of the very last employer; and all names and addresses of all employers for the last 19 months if the employee worked outside of the State of California.

Eligibility for Unemployment Insurance Benefits

In order to receive benefits, employees must be: 1) Able to work, 2) Available to work, and 3) Actively seeking work.

No benefits are possible if an employee voluntarily quits a job (unless it is for certain justifiable legal reasons), voluntarily retires, is discharged for deliberate misconduct, loses work because of a trade dispute, refuses to take suitable work, fails to make reasonable efforts to get work, makes false statements or withholds information.

Weekly benefits may be paid for 26 weeks or until the employee has received half of his or her annual wages, whichever is less. The first week of a claim is the waiting period and no benefits can be paid. All unemployment transactions begin with the Sunday of the week the employee calls in the claim. Claims are valid for one year. Every two weeks, a claimant must submit a new claim form to the EDD. An employee is urged to file a claim immediately, since retroactive benefits are rarely granted by the EDD. Depending on an employee's weekly pay, the maximum amount of an unemployment insurance benefit is $230 per week or $5,980 for 26 weeks.

How to File a Disability Insurance Claim

Claimants should obtain a claim form from the nearest EDD office. This can be done by telephone or letter. A form may also be obtained from the claimant's doctor or hospital. The form should be filled out and given to the claimant's doctor to complete. The claim must be filed no later than the 41st day after the first day for which benefits are payable. Depending on the claim, the maximum amount an employee may collect is $336 per week or $8,736 per year. Claimants should also evaluate private disability benefits from an employer, which may be better.

Eligibility for Disability Insurance Claim

Disability Insurance is payable when an employee cannot work due to illness or injury not caused by the job or if the employee is entitled to workers' compensation at a rate less than the daily benefit amount for disability insurance. Benefits may begin either with the day after the seven-day waiting period of disability or with the first day of hospitalization, whichever comes first. An employee may be paid for the waiting period if the disability exceeds 14 days.

Hearing Impaired

A phone number for the hearing impaired is (800) 735-2929.

APPENDIX D

Free Additional Employee Rights Information

Additional publications and services on employee rights are available. Call (800) 774-7494 or (949) 380-0900, or visit Mr. Sessions' office at 23456 Madero, Suite 170, Mission Viejo, CA 92691.

Articles, books, audio tapes and videos: Many free resources on employee rights are available by visiting Mr. Sessions' office. They include hundreds of his published articles, a large, easy-to-understand book collection, and scores of audio tapes and videos.

Phone Review: Call (949) 733-4242 for a taped review of employee rights by Mr. Sessions.

Website: Visit Job-law.com to request a free monthly newsletter or access comprehensive published articles on employee rights, including: a) Win when you lose—Ten job loss benefits, b) Broken prom-ises, c) Evaluating your case, d) At-will employment, e) Wrongful termination, g) Ten myths at work, g) Severance pay, h) Whistleblower rights, i) Discrimination options, j) Sexual harassment, k) Discrimination: Do you have a case?, l) Wrongful termination: Your rights, and m) Looks discrimination.

Seminars: Mr. Sessions or another attorney presents a 90 minute multi-media seminar on employee rights every Wednesday at noon. You will have a chance to ask the attorney any question. The usual fee is waived if you mention this book.

Radio: Mr. Sessions analyzes current employee rights topics on a half-hour radio program every month. Call his office for the broadcast time and station.

COPYRIGHTS

INDEX

Order Form

Call toll free and order now

Telephone: (800) 774-7494
Fax: (949) 380-8283
E-Mail: PretiumPress@Job-law.com
Postal: Pretium Press
23456 Madero, Suite 170
Mission Viejo, CA 92691

Please send me _____ copy/copies of *Employee Rights in California*

Name: _____

Address: _____

City: _____ State: _____

Zip: _____ Telephone: (___)_____

BOOKS	COST	TOTAL
One copy	$14.95	$14.95
Additional copies	$10.95 ea.	$
CA sales tax*	7.75%	$
Shipping: first copy additional copies	$3.20 $2.00 ea.	$
TOTAL		$_____

* If shipped to a California address

Payment Method:

Check___ VISA___ MasterCard___ Discover___AMEX___

Card No.:_____ Exp. Date_____ / _____

Name on card:_____